Retool Your Relationship

Retool Your Relationship

Fix the One You're With

TRINA DOLENZ

WILEY

John Wiley & Sons, Inc.

Published by John Wiley & Sons, Inc., Hoboken, New Jersey
Published simultaneously in Canada

Page 32: Illustration by John and Sue Laverack reprinted with permission.

For general information about our other products and services, please contact our Customer Care Department within the United States at (800) 762-2974, outside the United States at (317) 572-3993 or fax (317) 572-4002.

Wiley also publishes its books in a variety of electronic formats. Some content that appears in print may not be available in electronic books. For more information about Wiley products, visit our web site at www.wiley.com.

ISBN 978-0-470-63355-7 (paper); ISBN 978-0-470-88047-0 (ebk); ISBN 978-0-470-88048-7 (ebk); ISBN 978-0-470-88049-4 (ebk)

Printed in the United States of America

10 9 8 7 6 5 4 3 2 1

This book is dedicated to my darling daughters, Charlotte, Emily, and Georgia, who are my inspiration, motivation, and joy. They have always been my best critics and my most solid support.

Contents

Acknowledgments   ix

INTRODUCTION   Relationship Rehab: Change His
Toolish Ways   1

PART ONE
Understand Your Tool   9

    SESSION 1   Connect with Your Tool   11

    SESSION 2   Break Past Patterns, Solve Present
Problems   38

    SESSION 3   Why Are You with Him?   64

PART TWO
Act Now to Retool Your Relationship   81

    SESSION 4   Romance and Intimacy: The Perfect
Balance   83

    SESSION 5   Arguing Effectively with Your Tool   105

    SESSION 6   Share Your Roles in the Relationship   124

SESSION 7   How to Deal with Your Tool's Cheating   148

SESSION 8   Sex: The Ultimate Power Tool   175

SESSION 9   Jealousy: Avoid a Three-Way Collision   200

PART THREE
Change to Retool Your Relationship   **223**

SESSION 10   Can You Commit? Or Is He Just a Tool?   225

Further Reading and Web Sites   243

References   245

Index   247

Acknowledgments

It's funny how a casual and unassuming comment spoken at the right time can be life-altering. In my case, a chance remark from my hairdresser about how I needed to follow my heart and fulfill my destiny truly resonated with me. At that moment, I knew with absolute certainty what it was I wanted to do with my life, and the very next morning I enrolled with Relate, the British nonprofit couples counseling organization, whose offices were just down the street from where I was living in Cambridge.

While practically unknown in the United States, Relate is widely familiar to most people living in the United Kingdom as that country's largest provider of relationship support, with over seventy years of experience and six hundred locations. Not only does Relate provide its clients with relationship psychotherapy, it also provides a rigorous program of study to therapists.

I completed my primary training, received my license from Relate, and moved to London where I set up a private practice as a member of the British Association for Counseling and Psychotherapy. I decided to continue with my training at the University of East London and obtained the Relate postgraduate diploma in couples psychotherapy. It was while I was enrolled in this advanced degree program that I was very fortunate to be taught and inspired by my wonderful course director, Jenny Riddells. Through her I was able to achieve a much deeper insight into the theories and techniques used to counsel couples. This postgraduate course made everything click and formed the foundation for this book.

Over the years, it became my strong conviction that understanding the dynamics that shape relationships and the ability to improve them needn't be limited to trained therapists. Quite the contrary, the insights and ability to address relationship problems could be made accessible on a larger scale and help greater numbers of people achieve an intimacy and honesty that had previously eluded them. I also knew that one of the best ways to reach an audience with this information was through television. That's when I headed for Los Angeles.

It was my good fortune to share this dream with Clive Pearse, an English friend who was the host of an HGTV show produced by 495 Productions, the same company that produces *Tool Academy*. He heard that 495 Productions needed a therapist to help anchor a new reality show aimed at transforming bad boyfriends into responsive partners. He generously put the owner and executive producer of 495 Productions, Sally Ann Salsano, and me together. She in turn championed me to VH1. The rest, as they say, is history.

I am very grateful to Jim Ackerman at VH1 for giving me the start to my television career with the opportunity of being the therapist on *Tool Academy*. By showing people how to retool their relationships, with enough humor thrown in to make it entertaining, millions of television viewers have gained insight into their own relationships.

Another way to share my unique therapeutic approach with a large audience is through the written word. And, again, it was quite by chance during the first season of *Tool Academy* that I was contacted by the Agency Group and asked if I would like to write a book about relationships. While the concepts and ideas for my book were already formulated, I needed help putting them in fluent English, rather than in my somewhat disjointed therapy speak! Perhaps it was also destiny to have Clair Watson, my dear friend, suggest that her husband, Marc Kaplan, take a look at my first draft. Fortunately for me, he possessed the sensitivity and talent to capture on paper the concepts and nuances of my therapeutic philosophy and deftly transpose my Britishisms into understandable American English. Marc has been a professional science and medical writer for over twenty years, having published articles and book reviews in the *New York Times, Psychology Today*, and the *Washington Post*. He also has a background in medical and health-care public relations and has held positions at Rockefeller University, Consumers Union, the Robert Wood Johnson Foundation, and the University of Pennsylvania. He helped me enormously in the writing and editing of this book, and I want to extend my heartfelt thanks to him for his steadfastness, encouragement, and enthusiasm.

I would like to thank Caroline Greeven and Marc Gerard at the Agency Group for realizing that a book based on *Tool Academy* held promise, and to Tom Miller at John Wiley & Sons for realizing that promise and giving me the platform to share my couples therapy with so many women and their partners.

Finally, I wish to thank all of my wonderful clients and cast members who so generously let me into the privacy of their relationships and who trusted me to help them at their most vulnerable moments. Each and every one of them gave back something of themselves, fortifying my commitment to help others and enriching me in the process.

Relationship Rehab: Change His Toolish Ways

Millions of viewers know me as the therapist of VH1's hit reality show *Tool Academy*. Before that, I had a thriving psychotherapy practice in London, where I helped hundreds of women find the satisfaction they felt was missing in their relationships. Over the years, I've sat down and talked with many women from all walks of life whose relationships with their boyfriends or husbands were in crisis. As I listened, it became clear to me that although my clients were clearly frustrated and miserable, their men would rather do anything, and I mean anything, to avoid discussing the fact that their relationships were in trouble. They spent more time in the office, they extended their workouts at the gym, they got busy with their hobbies or the chores they had previously neglected around the house. In short, they grasped at any diversion that would help them avoid confronting the problems that hovered like rain clouds in their relationships.

These women discovered the hard way one of the main tenets of "toolishness." Despite their men's ripped physiques and smooth talk, most guys are wimps when it comes to dealing with any sort of unpleasantness in their relationships. They are desperate simply to be left alone, in complete and carefree denial, even though they know their partners are unhappy, dissatisfied, or just plain fed up.

It's what you'd expect from a Tool. The meaning of "Tools" is very clearly defined to me by the women on *Tool Academy*. Of course, their men don't know they are Tools until they enter the academy gates, but we see quite quickly that they are not really the devils that their girlfriends label them as; instead, they are mostly insecure, unhappy, and confused guys who are trying to live up to their idea of being a man. To summarize the common definitions of a Tool: men who are annoyingly selfish and infuriatingly self-centered. They have enormous egos and believe themselves to be irresistible to women. Tools are usually very poor communicators and even worse listeners, except when it comes to listening to the sound of their own voices. Their philosophy in life is simple and could be tattooed on their foreheads: I'd Rather Be Partying. For a Tool, life is one big conga line, and he's at the front of it, oblivious to everyone and everything. Tools are often dishonest, too, but it's as if they can't help themselves. Lying to themselves, as well as to their partners, is part of keeping up their carefree, rock-'til-you-drop attitude. If you want to see a Tool break out in a sweat, just use the word "responsibility" in a sentence. Tools are extremely uncomfortable with the idea that they are accountable for their behavior.

You Can Do It on Your Own

More often than not, we women are the keepers of relationships. We can tell you when everything in the relationship is going smoothly, and we're the first to sense when something has gone horribly wrong. We're also the first ones to want to take action for change.

Unfortunately, our partners are typically not as able, willing, or pro-active as we are. Most men would prefer to zone out than confront a problem with their relationships head on. As a result, many women are burdened with the feeling that despite knowing what they want, they are stuck in a relationship they feel powerless to alter.

The bad news is that up until now, you probably felt trapped, helpless, and doomed to spend the rest of your life in relationship hell. The good news is, all of that is about to change. By working through this book's ten-session program, you are declaring that you are no longer willing to wait for your man to "agree" to work on the relationship. You acknowledge that preserving the status quo is no longer an option you are willing to accept. You've made up your mind that things in your love life have got to be different. And now you are on your way, about to make the necessary changes happen, on your own, without his permission, his agreement, or even his knowledge.

My *Tool Academy* Approach

This book offers you a step-by-step guide to help you resolve conflicts in your relationship with the man you believed was the answer to your dreams. The core concept is this: if you tell your man you want him to change, he's just going to dig his heels in and refuse. If, however, you understand and secretly manipulate the rules of the game, his behavior will likewise be altered, and you'll get the change you desire in your man.

The focus of the series *Tool Academy* is mostly centered on the male member of the couple, and we do that with resounding success. But as the show progressed, I made a key observation: a change in perspective, attitude, or behavior in one partner prepares the way for dramatic breakthroughs in the actions of the other. I've seen this time and time again. When one member of the couple starts to communicate more directly and honestly, the other is finally free to calm down and set aside any anger and resentment. This enables the individual to listen and understand his or her partner's position more clearly. Whether the end result is a stronger relationship or a shared understanding that the relationship is over, active communication is the essential ingredient to achieve a satisfying and sustainable love life. In short, control the communication, and you control the direction of the relationship. This book takes that premise and runs with it.

Changing the Rules of the Game

In my therapy practice, I work with clients to help them understand the rules of the game by controlling the emotional and behavioral forces at play in their relationships with their partners. Armed with this wisdom, women are able to make subtle (and sometimes not-so-subtle) changes in their communication that trigger desired responses in their lovers. I have adapted this proven approach so that you, the reader, can achieve the same results without entering into formal therapy. And the beauty of it is that your boyfriend may not even be overtly aware of why the relationship is changing for the better.

Another observation that continually impressed me on the set of *Tool Academy* is the strength of the women I've had the privilege of helping. They have resources and self-confidence in abundance, just lying beneath the surface. And that's what this book is also about, helping you tap into your natural strength and use the emotional resources that are your birthright to get what you truly want.

Sometimes it is simply enough to feel confident about your own feelings, to understand them and know that they are real and truly yours. It's the starting point of this book and our therapy together. That's because this belief alone can help trigger a shift in your style of interaction or the way you approach a problem. The result will be that your partner will have no alternative but to respond differently as well. And so your journey toward a more fulfilling and sustainable relationship is off and running. As long as you're ready to take a good, hard look at yourself, your partnership, and your past, you will be able to bring about the change you desire and deserve.

For those of you who know me from watching how I help troubled couples on *Tool Academy*, you already know that my style is firm but empathic, straight to the point, as well as caring. And I'm always on target when I assess the mess the couples find themselves in and how they can get out of it.

Yet what you see on the show is only a tiny portion of the interactions I have with the *Tool Academy* couples. I spend hours with them during the course of the season, working with them to confront their fears, encouraging them to understand what's beneath their frustration and anger.

The constraints of a one-hour reality series don't allow you— the viewer—to see everything that goes into the therapy sessions with the couples. Practically speaking, only a small fraction of the work I do with these couples ever makes it to the final cut. That's one reason I wrote this book. I wanted to give you an opportunity to benefit from what I do to help couples on the television program. In these pages, I explain many of the ideas and concepts that I incorporate into my therapy with participants on the show. You'll get a chance to engage in the exercises and the activities that have been refined through my experience and that of others who are well established in the field of couple therapy. You will come away with an understanding of how I approach and resolve problems in troubled relationships, such as lack of intimacy and trust, immaturity, and poor communication. As you work your way through the sessions—each chapter can be seen as one therapy session—you'll benefit most from my therapeutic style and technique if you think of yourself as me, the therapist, because we'll be working as a team, with me guiding you every step of the way.

Getting What You Want

The course of therapy presented in the book will at times be challenging, yet you will gain many insights and often have fun doing the exercises. Every session addresses a different problem in a troubled relationship and includes several activities to provide you with the skills you need to redistribute the flow of control toward you, the woman. You will find practical lessons on manipulating a conversation so that he really, and I mean really, listens; on getting him to treat you the way you want to be treated in sensitive social situations where you feel particularly vulnerable; on maneuvering a white-hot argument to a cooler, more rational level of discussion; and on leveraging sex to get him to be a more responsive, appreciative, and attentive lover.

The exercises in each session are highly focused, down-to-earth, and no-nonsense. These quizzes, questionnaires, and other activities will give you the necessary tools to refurbish your relationship so that you can experience the love you have been missing.

Your Tool Kit

Don't think that if you read this book, your relationship will magically improve. In order for meaningful and sustainable progress to unfold in your relationship, I'm asking you to commit to an organized agenda of exercises. These activities will provide you with tools for your tool kit, the accessories that you require to fix your relationship and prompt your man to display the feelings of love and affection that have gone missing. The exercises also happen to be enjoyable and immeasurably rewarding. They require nothing more than a few objects that you can easily find around the house. One item that you'll use during your journey will be a notebook. It doesn't matter what size or whether it's fancy or plain, but it's important that you keep your notebook in a private place because what you write in it is intended for you and you alone. This notebook will be your companion during the ten sessions, an important part of your tool kit.

For those of you who are familiar with *Tool Academy*, you know that each episode is structured around a specific attribute or characteristic, such as trust or communication, that I feel is an essential ingredient for a stable and healthy relationship. On the program, when a Tool succeeds in clearly and sincerely expressing that week's particular theme, he is given a Tool Academy badge, which permits him to stay in the academy for another week, advancing him to the next level, where he'll either demonstrate another essential quality of an honest and caring partner or be expelled.

Although the work we are going to do to whip your partner into shape will be a bit different from the sessions I have with couples on the TV show, the underlying concept of being rewarded for hard work and successful change is still crucially important. Naturally, I cannot be with you physically to present you with a badge as you accomplish the tasks that bring you closer to controlling your man's behavior and achieving the kind of relationship you desire. So, as you successfully complete each session in this book, I'll remind you to reward yourself. It could be giving yourself a day off from work, a chocolate sundae from your favorite sweet shop, or a luxurious bubble bath. It doesn't matter how big or how small the reward is, as long as you present yourself with something a bit out of the ordinary and that you acknowledge your passage from one level to the next.

. . . .

Open Your Notebook

For your first exercise, I suggest that you plan for success by listing in your notebook ten rewards you can give yourself as you work through each session in the book. Remember, it can be something as small as taking a taxi home from work instead of the bus or something a bit more extravagant, such as a new pair of shoes or a trip to the salon. Fantasize now about how you would like to congratulate yourself as you progress toward your goal. It is important that you itemize how you will pat yourself on the back before you begin each session. Clearly and unmistakably, the true reward is turning your Tool into a loving, responsible, and intimate partner, and I'll be there to guide you. As I've found in my practice, a little encouragement along the way—a pat on the back, a high five, or an enthusiastic "well done"—is always appreciated.

• •

The real ingredient for success is you. What you bring to this challenge will determine how far and how deep your relationship will change for the better. Your participation, using the ideas presented in this book and the exercises outlined in each session, is the key determinant of your success in achieving a more meaningful and sustainable level of intimacy. After all, you wouldn't expect to lose weight simply from reading a diet book, would you?

You may not know it, but you have already started on the road toward positive changes. Merely reading and thinking about the tasks I have briefly described in this introduction have put you in what I call the "observer position," or "having a relationship about your relationship." Insights that flow from this stance will give you the perspective you need to take your relationship to a new level, if that is what you choose to do.

By the end of our time together, you will have single-handedly altered the course of your relationship and created an environment where you are in better control of how you and your partner can work together to achieve the change and growth you desire.

After all, your man is only human. He really does want to please you and actually wants what you want. He's hurting, too, although he won't admit it. He's just making more of a mess of things than usual and maybe he is a bit more in the dark than you are and probably a lot more inept about finding the light at the end of the tunnel. In the final analysis, this course of therapy offers a way for you to take control of the forces within the relationship to get what you want, thereby also helping him get what he wants. Which is, after all is said and done, you!

PART ONE

Understand
Your Tool

· ·

Connect with Your Tool

Let's chat. You are having problems with your man. Do you wonder how a relationship that was once stable and secure could turn so rocky and rough? What happened to the man you once found so intriguing and who was so interested in you? Now you can barely endure his endless patter at the dinner table as he rattles on about his day at work. And if he stops his self-absorbed monologue long enough to ask about your day, he can barely mask his indifference when you answer. Yet you persist, giving it your best shot and enlivening the details with amusing quips. Before you've even finished, though, he's crawled into his shell, with all of his attention focused on his food.

And since we're having a bitchfest, when exactly did the life of the party become such a bore in bed?

You've done plenty to maintain the relationship—keeping him together emotionally and perhaps even financially—and what you are now going through is definitely not what you bargained for. The women I've worked with often express feelings of betrayal during the course of their therapy when they realize that their men aren't giving them the care and the love they require for happiness and fulfillment. Women who find themselves in this predicament tell me that they feel duped, fooled (not necessarily sexually, although that can also be the case), and taken in by their guy's phony promises, sweet talk, or scheming charm.

Often these women come to me as a last resort, after they've tried everything else to salvage their relationships. They've confronted their partners with their feelings. They have taken the advice of parents, friends, and Internet relationship gurus. Sometimes the girl has tried buying the guy gifts, going on a romantic vacation, making friends with his friends, letting him always choose the movie and the restaurant when they go out on the weekend, all to no avail. He wears a disappointed smile when he opens his present; the vacation is torture, an ordeal where they fight over every little thing; he acts embarrassed and apologetic when she hangs out with his friends; and he barely makes eye contact with her when they go out on a date.

How could something that was once so right go so terribly wrong?

Relationship Types

No two relationships are ever entirely alike, for the obvious reason that no two people are alike. Yet it's also true that even though all troubled relationships begin and evolve differently, by the time they end up at my door, they often share many of the same characteristics. I'm sure you can recognize some of the following relationship types.

BABES IN THE WOODS

For example, some couples are like Babes in the Woods. They are called that because they behave like two innocent and inexperienced lovers, hiding under a blanket and totally absorbed in each other. They are having such a good time that they don't notice they are actually lost in a forest. They probably got together sexually pretty fast, enjoy a very active sex life, and feel very turned on about how good they are together in bed. They believe they don't have any problems of their own. When they see problems in someone else's relationship (and they do all the time), they feel a kind of self-affirmation that their relationship is special. The magic of their relationship is strengthened by the disenchantment they feel about their friends' and family members' relationships.

Yet in reality, they do have problems. As is inevitable with any couple, they might become annoyed, bored, or disappointed with each other, but they keep their disillusionment well hidden, not only from each other but from themselves as well. What typically happens is that one member of the couple pokes his or her nose outside the blanket and recognizes that something worthwhile exists outside their relationship. It could be the desire to make more friends or pick up a hobby. Perhaps the man decides to take more courses for work or the woman wants to further her career by going back to college. Regardless of the activity, it lies outside the relationship and therefore threatens the other member in the couple, who is still trying to maintain the magic.

The crisis comes to a head for these Babes in the Woods when the excluded member of the couple becomes threatened and anxious. Feeling disconnected from the relationship, this person looks around at the unfamiliar, alarming territory, panics, and tries to find some way back to exclusivity and safety.

IDOL AND FAN

Another common type of relationship that can signal trouble for a couple is labeled "Idol and Fan" by therapists. Usually, the role of the Idol is played by maverick nonconformists who like to do things their way, in their own time, with their own inimitable style. These people may be artists or musicians or may work in promotions at a nightclub. Perhaps the Idol is a talented mechanic or a graphic designer or a landscaper who likes the freedom of working outside the confines of an office environment, on his or her own schedule.

The Fan is an admirer, someone who is happy to bask in the reflected glory of the Idol. The Fan believes that by being in close proximity to the Idol, some of the popularity, adoration, or glamour will rub off and put a shine on the Fan, who feels boring, dull, and mundane.

Although it was thrilling for these two to be together at the beginning of the relationship, at some inevitable point the glitter begins to fade and serious problems surface between the Idol and the Fan. This is when the Idol begins to disappoint the Fan. Whether the lucky break never materializes, the Idol is fired from his or her job, or this person merely doesn't live up to expectations, he or she falls off the pedestal, leaving the Fan disillusioned, isolated, and disoriented.

CAT AND DOG

There are several other scenarios I've grown accustomed to seeing in my years as a therapist. For example, with the Cat and the Dog, a couple's entire relationship is based on their bickering with each other, but they don't usually break up permanently. They appear to thrive on their battles, feeling that their lives would lack an element of emotional intensity without the strife. The Cat and the Dog become used to their fighting as a form of intimacy.

Their problems come to a flash point when one member of the relationship gets sick and tired of the nonstop fighting and has a desperate feeling that life is going in circles. Yet there is an incredibly tight connection between these two people, and therapists are challenged to help them make significant changes. If they do decide to separate, it's often only to get back together again and resume where they left off.

MASTER AND SLAVE

Then there is the Master and the Slave, a relationship based on power struggles. It is often displayed by the guy using money to exert control and the girl using sex as her currency. The bubble often bursts when the woman starts to make enough money to threaten her man's bargaining power. I'll show you how to use your sexual power to take control of the relationship dynamics in session 8.

PURSUER AND DISTANCER

The Pursuer and the Distancer is a relationship scenario I'm sure you'll recognize. It's one of the most common dynamics and is found in even the happiest, healthiest relationships. Because many therapists acknowledge that it is so integral to conflicts in relationships, I've made it one of the central themes of my therapeutic approach.

No matter how blissful or fulfilling a relationship starts out, at some point one member of the couple—usually, the woman—begins to feel twinges of dissatisfaction, disappointment, or just plain unhappiness. She'll express her feelings openly, attempting to get her partner to acknowledge that something has changed in the relationship, that something needs to be done to get it back on track. She pursues her man with the goal of getting him to give her emotional reassurance and provide a closer sense of intimacy.

A man and a woman naturally go in and out of emotional sync with each other during the course of their relationship. It's a normal and very common occurrence, and many couples are able to work through it. But trouble sets in when the woman articulates her feelings of loneliness and her requirements for increased intimacy, and her man responds by distancing himself. He shuts down, pulls away, and coils up tighter than ever in his shell. He might respond by simply denying his partner, telling her that what she says is blatantly untrue. He may deflect her attempts to initiate a dialogue by changing the topic, injecting a bit of humor, and even expressing anger or hurt surprise. He may say that he's busy at the moment and that he'll talk to her later.

One basic skill you need to retool your relationship is the ability to reverse roles, so that instead of your constantly pursuing him, he'll start to pursue you. Simply put, it all comes down to taking control of the communication in the relationship.

Remember that most balanced relationships contain elements of all five of these couple types. In many couples, the guy and the girl are able to dip in and out of these roles frequently, but trouble brews when they get stuck in one particular mode.

Speaking Different Languages

After a few sessions in my therapy room, my clients usually discover that they don't speak the same language. They think they do because of how they communicated when they first fell in love. They were so in tune with each other that they hardly needed to say anything to know what the other one meant. They had formed a temporary "in love" language, in which both of them felt understood and heard. They remember these early days of their relationship as pure bliss and are stunned when they notice that they are not on the same communication wavelength as before. The couple thinks that their crisis is due to their inability to turn back the clock and relive the intensely romantic period of their early relationship, when communication was easy and unforced.

The reality of the situation is quite different. The truth is that many couples in this predicament are in trouble not because they have lost the ability to communicate like starry-eyed lovers, but because they are facing the real work of the relationship, a struggle that they are destined to repeat over and over until hopefully resolved (more about that later).

Men hear things differently than women do. Men also tend to respond differently but in predictable ways that you can cleverly leverage to get yourself heard. It's all in how you communicate. Yet before you can learn new ways to communicate to achieve the results you want, let's explore how you've been communicating and receiving communications up to this point. And that begins with shifting your perspective from being an active participant to being an observer of your own relationship.

I understand full well that you inhabit your relationship so entirely that it has become part of the very air you breathe. For you to step away and observe it objectively would be like playing an intense game of volleyball on the field and refereeing the action at the same time. I grant you, it is difficult but not impossible, and the results will be a gratifying revelation to you.

Become an Observer in Your Relationship

The fact is, you know how to observe relationships because you've been watching them most of your life. The following exercise using your journal will help you sharpen your observational skills and read between the lines to interpret the hidden meanings.

• •

Open Your Notebook

Think back to when you were younger and try to recall a situation in which you witnessed your parents having a conversation or even an argument. Remember what was being said and try to remove any emotional associations you have with the exchange. Just think about how it was said and what you could tell was happening underneath all of the words. Open your notebook, and, in a few short sentences, write down what you recall being said. You are simply transcribing the conversation as you remember it; resist adding any emotional interpretation you might associate with the words you write down.

Now I'd like you to fast-forward to the last time you were out with another couple or friends and had the opportunity to observe their dialogue. Put on your detective cap and recall their body language, the tone and the inflection of their verbal exchanges, and their choice of words. Write down this dialogue in your notebook just as you remember it. As you reread this entry, notice how often the two speakers interpreted—or misinterpreted—what was said and how it shaped their response.

● ●

To give you more insight into the subtext of a conversation, here's an example of an overheard conversation between a couple in a restaurant:

She (watching as her boyfriend reaches over and helps himself to a forkful of her french fries): Hey, wait a minute! Why not ask for a bite before just taking one?
He (laughingly): You're so stingy. It wouldn't hurt you to share once in a while.

Seems harmless enough, right? But in that brief exchange, you may have noticed that their four-sentence dialogue contained a wealth of possible clues hinting at a set of dynamics at play just below the surface of their relationship. Now, it would be understandable if you said that all she required of her boyfriend was the courtesy of being asked for a bite of her meal before he helped himself to it. But perhaps this type of behavior is one of her major pet peeves; it reminds her of the way her brother used to pick food off her plate and disrespect her in other obvious and not-so-obvious ways. It is also possible that the boyfriend knows that this behavior will drive his girlfriend up the wall. Perhaps he's getting back at her for keeping him waiting downstairs in the car, or maybe he's angry with her about something far more serious. Regardless of the provocation, he is clearly stung by her words, so much so that he goes on the attack and turns up the temperature by criticizing her and making a negative and quite sweeping comment about her personality.

So you see, something as simple as a few words of conversation can open a window into a couple's deeply personal world and provide a peek at the forces at work in their relationship.

Here's another example of how people in a relationship often interpret the same words very differently, based on their past experiences. Even though their different interpretations often lead to an unpleasant or even explosive episode, the man and woman continue to carry on in the relationship as if they believe the other person has ESP.

Let me introduce you to a couple I have worked with in the past, Marcia and Randy. Marcia recently received a promotion at work and called her boyfriend, Randy, to tell him the good news. He responded just as she hoped he would by suggesting that they celebrate by having a "date night at home." As she pocketed her cell phone, Marcia summoned up images of candles and wine, quiet conversation, and a fabulous dessert. But when she got home, she discovered that he had ordered pizza and one of his favorite DVDs.

Marcia was hurt and felt let down. When she tried to bring up why she felt so disappointed, Randy simply couldn't understand what had put Marcia into such an unappreciative and ungrateful mood. In Marcia's family, special occasions were marked by dinner around the table, with everyone chatting amicably, surrounded by good food and hearty laughter. For Randy, family celebrations usually centered around the TV, with everyone watching sports, as friends and neighbors dropped by, got something to eat, and lounged contentedly on sofas and chairs. The situation might have been prevented if Randy asked what Marcia might like to do to celebrate and let her dictate the particulars of the evening. Randy simply assumed they were on the same page.

This example illustrates how a couple can spend much of their time misunderstanding each other if they don't invest time in learning how to effectively communicate.

Emotional Echoes from Your Past

Marcia and Randy's story also demonstrates how experiences from a distant past can affect your daily life and present relationship. Often, arguments in a relationship stem from something your man says or does that reminds you of an earlier painful or unhappy experience. You then react to these negative associations by feeling upset, fearful, or just plain pissed off.

When many of my clients begin therapy, they are caught up in reacting instinctively to these hidden emotional scars. They blindly charge down the path of rage and resentment without being aware that these emotions are but memories of a painful situation that happened to them long ago. In therapy, however, they learn that they have a choice when these emotions tug on their sleeves. By stopping to understand what is going on beneath the surface, rather than misinterpreting it, they can break their bonds with the past.

Who hasn't experienced a situation in which your man says something that reminds you of what your parents or a family member used to say to you, which causes you to feel hurt or inadequate? In one extreme case, a woman flew into a rage when her boyfriend, watching her put on mascara and lipstick and wishing to give her a compliment, said that she was so attractive already that any extra effort would be "useless." Later, I learned that my client had consistently been put down as a teenager by her envious mother whenever she applied makeup in the mirror before going on a date. Her mother had told her that trying to make herself look attractive was "useless." Her boyfriend's attempt at a compliment (clumsy though it may have been!) triggered all of her past feelings of inadequacy and resentment. If she had known how to observe herself and interpret the comment as it was intended, she could have channeled her hurt feelings more appropriately, rather than taking them out on her boyfriend in a nasty fight.

In another example, could the way your boyfriend repeatedly instructs you how to drive remind you of the times when your mother tried to teach you to drive and ended up yelling at you? If this is the case, it's easy to see why you might lash out at him when he reminds you to use your turn signal when you are about to pass the car in front of you.

And what's with him texting all the time? Whenever you try to have a conversation with him, he pulls out his phone and starts tapping away to one of his friends about nothing very important, while you're standing right there, trying to get his attention! Does it remind you of your father, who always had the television on when you tried to talk to him about school and kept watching sports or a sitcom—anything that was on, really—instead of paying attention to you?

Disarm, Listen, Check It Out!

Learning to listen objectively to what you hear is an essential skill in controlling communication to achieve your emotional goals. You and your boyfriend did this with each other when you first met, but then there were no barriers between you, and you both used the same language. Now your relationship is in crisis, the two of you speak different languages, and you're wearing your armor, ready to fight or defend yourself. I will show you how to listen, speak his language, check things out, and use all of the communication tools that will be in your tool kit to disarm, retool your relationship, and ultimately get what you want.

• •

Open Your Notebook

Open your notebook and write down three instances when you reacted emotionally to your man. It doesn't matter right now who was right or wrong in the situation. All that is important is that you felt swept up by a strong emotion, whether it was anger, humiliation, or maybe shame. Be sure to write down what was said before you reacted and how you reacted. It's not important to link that emotion with a past experience or a family member. Right now, your goal is to sensitize yourself to your and your partner's style of communication, to learn to listen objectively to what you hear.

• •

Listening to our men is often one of women's weaker skills because we are so accustomed to being passive or agenda-oriented when we listen. For couples who have been together for a substantial period of time, real conversation can be a challenge. How many times can you listen to your man tell you the same stories over and over again before you stop listening altogether? His days of glory playing high school sports? His trip to Fort Lauderdale during spring break when he got so drunk he left the car running in the middle of the street and woke up the next morning unable to remember where he'd left it? And when he's had a bad day at work, he just won't let it go: his dumb boss or the idiots he works with or the crazy customers. After two or three of these monologues, you can tell what he's going to say before he says it.

EXERCISE

Pipe Down and Listen

Many men and women I see in therapy have stopped listening to one another long before they reach my office. That's why in this next exercise, you will do a lot of active listening. By this, I mean you will suspend any judgment or evaluation, as you probe what your man says with short, neutral questions that are designed to help him come out of his shell a bit and feel safe to express himself, perhaps with previously unarticulated thoughts or feelings.

You will probably hear things—a tone of voice, perhaps—that you haven't heard in a long while or perhaps ever. It may even rekindle an appreciation for your guy, which has been on a very low flame for a long time.

To accomplish this feat, you will need to pipe down and listen for ten minutes, once a day, and let him do most of the talking. Let him go on about his day, his commute, his mother, your mother, and all the while you are listening, saying very little, taking it all in.

The real work of this exercise is that I'd like you to pretend to be me—the therapist! You have seen therapists played on television and in the movies to know just enough about how they act: Inquisitive but accepting. Probing but respecting of boundaries. Sympathetic but without giving obvious approval. A lot of head nodding and "How does that make you feel?" It's also a bit like playing a detective. You will sound curious and interested—not in a "Gotcha!" way, but as if you are genuinely empathizing with his experience and want to learn more.

As with most survival routines that couples have carved out for themselves, however, you'll need to unlearn some old habits. The kinds of questions I'd like you to ask as the therapist are those that check out what is actually being said. Use phrases that encourage him to give you details. Don't settle for the kind of answers you usually get when you ask him what his day was like. If he answers, as he always does, "Nothin' special," don't stop there. Show him that you are sincerely interested. Use your knowledge of his life to get him to open up. Because you know he has a long commute, ask him how it went today. Because you have heard him complain about his new colleague, ask him how it's working out. Be curious. Care about his answers.

Also, in this exercise, I'd like you to reflect his responses back to him by repeating what you've heard. Be quite certain that you've heard him correctly. Here's an example. Him: "I had to stand around all day while my boss showed the new guy the ropes." Now, you could have responded by saying, "Why didn't you just tell your boss that you'd show the new guy the ropes?" Or, "Sounds like your boss doesn't think much of your time to waste it like that." Or even, "That sounds just like something your boss would do." Instead, however, I want you to simply reflect back what he has said and what you have heard, using his own words as much as possible. In this case, it might go something like this. You: "Sounds like you had a hard day just standing around your boss!"

Here's another example. Him: "Billy wimped out again and didn't make the game. His girlfriend has him by the balls." You might feel the urge to go on the offense, defend his girlfriend and suggest that maybe Billy had better things to do than hang out at a ballgame with the same bunch. Maybe you don't like Billy and see an opportunity to get a dig in and agree that Billy is indeed a big wimp and not only for passing up the ballgame with the boys. Instead, I want you to listen carefully and mirror your response based on your guy's comment. You can try saying something like, "Too bad he missed the game. Sounds like he disappointed every-one." Now here is an opportunity to play the therapist, probe a bit to get more details, and be curious. You might follow up with, "Does it happen often that his girlfriend prevents him from going to the game?" Or maybe, "Can you remember a time when she prevented him from joining up with you before?"

Try to use questions that need more than a yes or no answer, so that he can continue to talk and feel as if he is being interest-ing. If you get stuck, simply summarize what he has said in your own words. Nod your head and follow up by asking a question to clarify what he is telling you. At no time add any of your own comments, judgments, advice. Simply listen, observe, and check back with him. Make sure that what you have heard is what he has said. It will feel a bit weird at first, stilted, false, or one-sided. All change feels awkward to begin with. This is an important skill for you to pop into your tool kit for later use. For now, its purpose is to let him know that you are really listening. As he begins to feel listened to, he will feel less threatened and disconnected from you, and you will have begun to prepare him for the lessons ahead.

The hard part of this exercise is not being able to express yourself and not engage in your side of the conversation. But remember, it's only for this session, and it is going to change him in the long run.

EXERCISE

Are You Really Listening?

For a quick assessment of how you rate yourself as a listener, copy the six questions below in your notebook and choose the response that describes you best: always, sometimes, rarely, never. This assessment will give you some ideas on how you can become a better listener in the future.

1. Do I interrupt?
2. Do I really listen "between the lines" when he says one thing but perhaps means something else?
3. Do I really concentrate and try to remember important information?
4. Do I have control of my emotions if he is angry or upset?
5. Do I turn off the TV/stop reading my book when he is talking?
6. Do I show him I am interested by giving eye contact and turning toward him?

Uncrossing the Wires

At first, try the Pipe Down and Listen exercise for a few days on very neutral topics, ones that don't push your buttons or set off any emotional fireworks. After you feel a bit more comfortable, try it on a more sensitive topic. Here's an example:

I was conducting a session with Margo and Tom, who were having communication difficulties. Margo's complaint was that she always felt criticized by Tom. I started them off by selecting a topic that I knew they were struggling with. Margo got upset that Tom always left the room or walked away from her when he was talking on the telephone. It made her feel suspicious, untrustworthy, even shut out.

> Tom: I think you are always trying to listen in on my private conversations. You're crowding me.
>
> Margo: I never listen to what you are saying. I really couldn't care less! But I don't understand why you can't say what you need to say in front of me. You are always talking to that buddy of yours. What are you saying to him that you don't want me to hear?
>
> Tom: Listen, I have a right to my privacy, and I can talk to whomever I want to, whenever I want to!

Margo and Tom were getting dangerously near the same flash point that they always reached when they brought up this topic. I intervened by helping them change the way they constructed their sentences. Then I let Margo start again.

> Margo: It really bothers me that you cannot talk on the phone in front of me.

This time, I asked Tom to repeat back to Margo what he had heard without putting any of his own thoughts or emotions into the reply.

> Tom: I am really sorry that you . . .
>
> Me: No, don't apologize. Just reflect back to Margo that you understand what she is having a problem with.

Tom: Okay. You don't like it when I go away from you when I talk on the phone. I *now* know it makes you feel anxious.

Me: Great! Margo, does that sum up how you feel?

Margo: Yes! I thought he did it deliberately just to piss me off! Tom, it's great to hear you understand that when you walk out of the room, you make me feel like you've got something to hide.

By reporting back what you have heard from the position of being an observer in the conversation, you will be able to help your man not only understand his feelings more clearly but also articulate them. Now your feelings are out in the open, and you can address them directly and honestly. It is up to Tom if he wants to continue to leave the room when he's having a telephone conversation. But my hunch is now that Margo knows that Tom knows how she feels, she'll be more comfortable letting him have private conversations with his friends on the telephone without her feeling suspicious or untrustworthy, and Tom will be more comfortable staying in the room while talking on the phone.

I hope that you are now beginning to appreciate how powerful you can be in a conversation when you participate as an observer of the communication. Let's try one more exercise where, by being the observer in a conversation, you can gain the control you need to achieve the balanced, healthy relationship you want.

Parent, Adult, and Child Roles

Have you ever caught yourself instructing or advising your partner about something and then you stopped and thought to yourself, Oh, my God! I sounded like my mother just then. We all have moments in a conversation when we sound like our parents: "Don't forget to bring an umbrella; it's going to rain later today." "You're trying to do too much; you're going to exhaust yourself and get sick."

"Don't stay out too late; remember, you have to get up early in the morning for that job interview." Whenever your sentences are full of "oughts" and "shoulds," you are taking on a parental role in the conversation.

It's not a bad thing to provide a parental perspective. You do so when you think you need to give nurturing advice or well-intentioned guidance. It might not be received in the spirit that it is given, but you are only trying to do what's best for your boyfriend. He may think you are nagging, overbearing, or being protective, and maybe you are, just a little.

We all occasionally sound like parents and children—and so we should, when it's appropriate. How annoying would it be, though, if you played the parental role and he the child every time the two of you made love? In this case, the best sexual environment is when you are both on the same level, preferably acting a bit like curious and carefree children.

There is a third communication role, however, through which you can have a meaningful conversation, and that is to speak as an adult. It's by communicating in a factual, unemotional way that permits the other person to hear what you are saying in an unthreatening fashion and helps him or her also respond as an adult. We feel more connected when we convey our true intentions and when we feel understood without any underlying power-based agendas on either side.

Here's an example of what I mean. In the following two groups, each person says the same thing but from a different role:

Child: I'm not lending you my keys; you always lose the things I give you or never give them back.
Parent: Now if I lend you my keys, will you remember to return them right away?
Adult: The last time you borrowed my keys, you forgot to return them.

Child: Every time I make special plans to go out to dinner with you, your brother has to tag along.

Parent: Your brother ought to have his own social life and not come tagging along with us every chance he gets.

Adult: This is the third time this month that your brother came out to dinner with us.

Communicating like an adult is the way we talk to friends and business acquaintances. The tone of the discourse lacks emotional imperatives, judgments, or juvenile passivity. It is the kind of communication that lets the listener have a choice and gives him or her options about what needs to be done next. The conversation is open-ended and respectful.

EXERCISE

Recognize the Roles That You Both Play

In this exercise, I want you to simply notice when you take on a more parental role and your guy's response to it. The point is not to criticize or berate yourself when you give him these directives or expressions of concern; simply observe and make note of them.

At the same time, I also want you to recognize when your man says things that make you think he is acting like a child. It probably happens during the course of a weekend more times than you care to count—for example, whenever he gives you a snappy reply or throws out a quick, terse response or acts like he's Mr. Know-It-All. "I heard you the first time!" "You don't need to shout, I'm not deaf." "I've done it a hundred times and don't need you to tell me how."

When he talks back like that, he's acting a bit defiantly, and who can blame him? He probably does remember that he said he'd pick up some take-out on the way home (but it wouldn't hurt to give him a reminder, now would it?). Men (and women) can also act like children in conversations by being sarcastic: "Yes, babe,

I did put the top on the toothpaste." "Yes, honey, I'll put on a clean shirt when we go out for dinner with your parents on Saturday." In either case, defiant or sarcastic, he is carrying on a conversation by playing the role of a child.

• •

Open Your Notebook

Bearing in mind the three channels of communication— parent, adult, and child—write down two or three verbal exchanges you had with your boyfriend every day for a week. Determine who is playing what role, and write that role down next to the sentence of dialogue as you remember it. Are you speaking as the parent and he as the child? Are you taking on the child's role, while he plays the part of the parent?

There is no right or wrong, because there are times when it is entirely appropriate—even necessary—for you to act in a parental fashion. For example, in situations where your man needs a bit of extra nurturing, such as when he's sick or had an extremely bad day. And there will be times when both of you are in the parental mode, helping each other sort through a problem or planning a big night out.

As you write down your conversations and assign roles to yourself and your partner, you'll see the value of speaking to each other as adults. You'll discover that these are the most satisfying and meaningful interactions you can have. They are the conversations in which the two of you discuss a topic without pushing each other's buttons. You clearly and factu- ally describe the situation without being directive or bossy, allowing your man to freely formulate his own opinion and plan of action.

I imagine that at the moment, your adult-to-adult commu- nications are few and far between. You're discovering that you are either acting like the critical parent all of the time to his wayward child or else playing the hurt child to his scornful, withholding parent.

For now, simply notice how you talk to each other. It's a first step toward becoming an observer, understanding your man and your relationship, and taking control.

• •

Sex Check-Up

I want to conclude this first session by helping you to begin thinking about sex in a new and very different way. Sex is the central part of any romantic relationship. Sometimes sex brought you into the relationship in the first place, the sheer physical *wow* of it. Other times, it's the only thing left in the relationship, after all else has withered and shriveled away. It can also be a big hole in the relationship when you're not getting any! Yet it is always a reliable barometer of what is happening in the rest of the relationship.

You might think sex is the last place where I would ask you to break away from the action and become an observer. But in order to have the quality and frequency of sex you desire, you'll have to take control of your lovemaking, too. And to do that, you'll need to understand the various phases of your sex cycle and observe how they affect the pleasure you have—or don't have. Because sex is the ultimate form of communication, only by observing these phases and recognizing where the problems lie will you be able to control your physical dialogue and achieve the intimacy you desire.

THE SEX WHEEL

To begin, visualize your life as a wheel. Imagine that the hub of the wheel is your sex life and the various spokes are the other parts of your life—the public part—your friends, family, job, finances, hobbies. Generally, how you hang out the rest of the time. If every part of your life is going well, all of the spokes will be the same length, and your wheel will roll along smoothly.

If your mother is sick, however, or you are having an argument with your best friend or work is horrible, then your wheel will be bent out of shape. One spoke will be of a different length, and you're in for a bumpy ride. And if your problems involve more than one spoke, the ride will get even rougher.

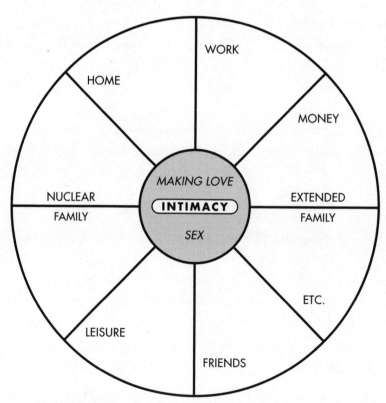

The sex wheel contains the various parts of your life. If everything is in balance, each spoke on the wheel will be the same length. Imbalances will cause the spokes to be uneven and will cause a bumpy ride.

• •

Open Your Notebook

Open your notebook and draw your sex wheel as it is now. Your wheel should have eight spokes, which represent work, money, home life, leisure, friends, you and your partner, extended family, and other areas you might want to add. Make the longer spokes the areas that are the healthiest. You'll quickly see that when the spokes are of equal length, your sex wheel will turn more smoothly. Don't worry, I certainly don't expect yours to look like a perfectly round wheel, as pictured on page 32, at the moment.

It may be that you are having trouble at work, which affects your sense of financial security. Or perhaps you have no social life, which influences how you spend your spare time. These are only two examples. If many of the spokes in your wheel are significantly different in length, your wheel will appear deflated. There will be little to support the hub, and your sex life is probably in serious trouble.

• •

YOUR SEX CYCLE

We will come back to the topic of sex time and again throughout this book and will handle it in depth in session 8. But for now, I'd like to acquaint you with what are well recognized as the five phases of lovemaking: desire, arousal, plateau, orgasm, and resolution.

• •

Open Your Notebook

To help you think about your sex cycle, I've created a questionnaire. In your notebook, answer each of the following questions thoroughly. Be honest and clear. This is for you and no one else. Let your imagination run free, relax all of your inhibitions, and don't let your answers be influenced by what you think your lover's reaction would be. These questions will help you see clearly how things are now and where you want to take them.

- What do you do to get your man in the mood?
- What does he do to get you in the mood?
- How do you indicate that you would like to take things further?
- How do you know whether your partner is up for it?
- Who takes the initiative?
- How easy is it to say no? What happens if you do say no?
- How do you know you are getting turned on?
- How do you know your man is beginning to get turned on?
- How easy is it for you to get turned off?
- How easy is it for you/him to get distracted?
- How easy is it to turn your man off?
- Do you/he plan for sex? Often, occasionally, never?
- How would you like to be seduced?
- How would you like to seduce your man?
- What are your fantasies?
- What are your man's fantasies?
- Does he know yours?

• •

SEXUAL DIFFERENCES BETWEEN MEN AND WOMEN

Sex has to start with desire. Something gets switched on inside of you, and there it is: you find your man attractive and you need contact. The expectation grows, and as you begin to kiss and touch each other, you both become increasingly aroused sexually.

Women need foreplay to become aroused, and their arousal usually takes longer than men's. Arousal will reach a plateau phase, which can be sustained for quite a while before orgasm occurs. I must mention here that it is rare for women to have orgasms from penetration alone, so if there is no or insufficient foreplay, then orgasm is unlikely.

It's different with a guy. He can get aroused and have an erection just by the sight or smell of you, a whispered word, or only your photograph. Also, when a man is on the path to orgasm, he is not able to control it as well as a woman can. There comes a point where his climax is inevitable, unstoppable, even if he does think of something to distract himself.

For women, achieving orgasm is also a state of mind and can be interrupted by a mere thought. After orgasm, there is a period of intimacy, closeness, freedom from stress, as you recover together from your climaxes; this is called the resolution period.

There are many ways to enjoy the phases of your cycle. Yet within each phase, there can also be problems that will stop your pleasure cold. One type of problem is that you and your lover are often not at the same part of the cycle at the same time. Another problem is that if you repeatedly have the same sexual issue at the same point in your sex cycle, then it will become increasingly more difficult for you to repeat the cycle. You may eventually stop having sex altogether, to avoid the inevitable, painful disappointment.

SEXUAL MIXED MESSAGES

Let me give you an example from *Tool Academy*. You might remember that one cast member said that whenever she and her partner had sex, immediately after orgasm he always got up and went into another room to watch TV. For this woman, there was no resolution phase of the cycle, none of the intimacy and closeness she required for a full, satisfying sexual experience.

What's more, this feeling of being abandoned also haunted her entire relationship. By winning a date night on the TV show and actually having sex, she admitted that it was the best sex ever because he could not escape when it was over. Because they were on television, you might think it would have been very awkward to have sex in public—so to speak. But the joy of being able to go through her complete sex cycle without the problems she usually had in the resolution phase was way more important than the idea that anyone else might be watching! By being on television, he simply couldn't escape and was forced to complete her cycle. Afterward, they lay together and talked and enjoyed sharing the experience. Later, in therapy, it became clear that they were both able to take pleasure in a newfound intimacy, which he admitted had brought them closer together.

Regarding another client whom I helped in my professional therapy practice, the woman was able to identify that she felt short-changed in the arousal period of her sex cycle. Her man rushed through it, foreplay was almost nonexistent, and their entire session was out of sync and unsatisfying. She never got fully aroused, he penetrated her very quickly, and because she was not sufficiently lubricated, it became rather painful and she consequently lost all interest in having sex. She knew that their cycle of lovemaking would lead to her feeling left behind and as if she had been used, and that it would always hurt! It's no wonder that she never wanted to start her sex cycle and was not able to feel desire for him.

Skillful Communication Is the First Step

Now that we've taken our first steps together, I hope you can begin to identify and understand the various modes and methods by which we communicate—and miscommunicate—with our lovers.

So much of what is wrong with your relationship revolves around messages being transmitted, verbally or nonverbally, that are unintentional and involuntary and that push the object of your desire further away from your grasp. That's why the perfect way to start retooling your relationship is to fully understand what you are communicating and to control how you communicate it. Communication is so closely bound up with behavior, and behavior tightly wrapped up in emotions, that by controlling how you communicate, you'll also be able to indirectly elicit the behaviors and the feelings you miss in your relationship.

You've already begun to master some very essential communication skills that you'll use during these ten sessions to steer your relationship in a direction toward greater fulfillment and intimacy.

An old Chinese proverb says that every journey begins with a first step. Congratulations! You've taken that first step, by learning how to control and improve your communication skills and those of your man. You are now able to identify the types of communication that steer your relationship right into a brick wall, and you can take the necessary steps to put on the brakes before the collision. It's hard work, I know, but all change is. If you were on *Tool Academy*, I'd award you the Communications badge. But for now, give yourself the first well-deserved reward you listed in your notebook.

Remember, the focus of this book is very much on improving the future of your relationship. Yet in order to do that, the next step along your path is to uncover some of the relationship hazards you're now exposed to, whose roots are buried in your past.

Break Past Patterns, Solve Present Problems

D o you have a girlfriend who always seems to end up with Mr. Wrong? Or maybe this even describes your love life. Is there an eerie similarity among the men you hook up with? Many of my clients had this problem when they first came to see me.

For example, take Samantha. Anytime that she and her boyfriend, Justin, went to a party or a bar, he would start hassling someone—usually, a guy twice his size—and the evening would end with a trip to the emergency room. Samantha spent more Saturday nights in the ER getting Justin bandaged than she cared to remember. She finally sought help in therapy when the ER doctors, seeing her week after week, began to treat her like a victim of the brawl.

Another of my clients—I'll call her Jaycee—always chose musicians as her boyfriends. Whenever they went out, she had to share her boyfriend with the other members of his band. At home, he'd reach for his guitar and start strumming every time she tried to have a conversation with him or, worse, right after sex. She referred to his guitar as the "other woman" in the relationship, until the real "other woman" inevitably showed up. All of her relationships ended when she discovered that her boyfriends were inveterate cheaters. She came to see me for help when she finally decided she had had enough.

Ami's boyfriends were all loners who liked to keep to themselves and preferred to stay at home. With her most recent boyfriend, the sex was great, but they were rarely together outside of the house. He seldom went out partying with friends or to a club. He never insisted that she stay home; he simply made it clear that he didn't like her friends. In the beginning of the relationship, on holidays like Halloween and the Fourth of July, she went to parties with her girl-friends (and their boyfriends), and he sat at home playing games on his computer. Ami began to feel guilty and then decline invitations to go out with her friends. She finally went into relationship therapy when she found herself all alone, again, harboring resentment toward him and missing the woman she once was.

Here We Go Again

It is easy to spot self-destructive or counterproductive patterns in other people's lives. With family members or longtime friends, we are able to recognize the recurring decisions and acts that somehow always end badly or get our loved ones into all kinds of trouble. These patterns can occur in any area, not only in their romantic lives. We can sometimes see when certain people repeatedly engage in behavior that pins them into a tight spot with their bosses, cowork-ers, or other friends, and we can predict they'll have a falling out. In each instance, something—usually, the same something—steps in to create a disaster that could have been avoided. It is much harder to recognize the destructive seeds that grow in our own relation-ships, blossoming into future disappointment, failure, or loss. After years of making the same bad choices in boyfriends, many of us finally begin to wake up to the fact that we can be our own worst enemies when it comes to selecting lovers. What is much harder to understand is why we are always attracted to the same type of guy. What compels us to court almost certain heartbreak? Why is it that we are drawn to the types of men who will inevitably hurt us by cheating or being emotionally distant or controlling, so that we never get what we truly need in a relationship? And once we are aware of the counterproductive forces that cloud our romantic judgment, how will we have the strength and conviction to open ourselves up to become romantically attracted to a different kind of person? Even worse, if we don't overcome our urge to seek out the wrong guy, we are continually doomed to be stuck in the messes we invariably find ourselves in.

Changing Your Past Patterns

This session will answer those questions. It is unlike any other session in the book because not only will it take you on a journey of discovery inside yourself, it also delves into your past. Many women whom I've helped have a strong reluctance to revisit their personal history. After all, they tell me, the past is dead and buried. They aren't interested in dredging up their childhood woes or old, unpleasant memories. Yet I know from experience that you will simply be unable to move forward in your relationship without confronting the events and relationships that shaped you, your desires, and your fears. You'll be left to do their bidding, reacting to emotions and incidents that occurred years ago, as you are hopelessly and repeatedly jerked around like a puppet on a string.

The exercises you'll do in this session are tactile, tangible, and concrete. They will probably be unlike anything you have ever tried before, so you will need to keep an open mind and be totally honest. If you stick with them, however, I guarantee that you will discover underlying patterns that have guided many key romantic decisions in your life—past and present. And you will learn how to break these patterns to make decisions based on what you truly want in a lover and a loving relationship.

It is only human nature to avoid pain, to shun the things that make us unhappy, and to shield ourselves from whatever makes us sad. Every one of us has, over the course of our lives, developed psychological or emotional shields we use to protect ourselves from painful memories and experiences and feelings of hurt and loss. We act on them every day of our lives, but we hardly take any notice, nor, for the most part, should we. These shields do their job quite successfully; they keep us functioning and protected, emotionally and psychologically safe. It's no wonder that psychologists call these psychic entities "defenses," because they do just that: they defend us from emotional and spiritual bruises so that we can carry on in our daily lives.

Yet there are times when these defenses outlive their welcome. At one point in your life, they were useful and helped you cope and adapt to new situations, but now they are obstacles, preventing you from getting to the emotional high ground by undermining your long-term self-interest. These defenses have hardened into patterns of self-destructive or counterproductive behavior that you repeat over and over again. The attitudes and feelings, shaped by relationships and people in your past, were totally understandable and beneficial at the time. But now they cast a giant shadow into your everyday life, and they invisibly control your behavior and reactions to situations without your being the least bit conscious of it.

The Myth That Opposites Attract

Let me tell you the story of Jody. She came into therapy because she so badly wanted to have a child, but each time she brought it up with her endless stream of boyfriends, they hemmed and hawed and eventually left her. It was clear to me from the moment we first met that she was desperate. She spoke loudly and forcefully, in a continuous flow of pressurized sentences that made it difficult for me to ask questions. As she related her story, she punctuated her speech with wild, expansive gestures that signaled to me how helpless she felt and in need of rescue. Her eyes darted from one corner of the room to the other. It was evident to me that Jody felt trapped and that time was running out. After listening for a while, I began to put the pieces together. Jody's primary complaint was that none of her boyfriends could commit to being fathers. We began to talk about what attracted her to certain men and about her choices of boyfriends. During the course of the session, she discovered that she found herself attracted to guys who acted fiercely independent and were rugged outdoor types, guys who liked to race bikes, fix cars, and run marathons—men who could take care of themselves.

Jody was an only child whose father worked in a large printing plant. He had long, irregular hours, and when he came home, her mother had doted on him hand and foot, drawing his bath for him, fixing his meals, making sure his clothes were clean. As a result, Jody felt as if she had been totally ignored. In fact, Jody had always been taught to dote on her father as well, and when her mother died of cancer, her father expected his nineteen-year-old daughter to step up and take care of him in the exact same way that his now-deceased wife had. Jody tried this for a while but then quite suddenly left home, and her father had to fend for himself.

Working with exercises such as the one I will introduce to you shortly, Jody discovered that the men she found attractive were those who—for one reason or another—thought of themselves only as permanent boyfriends, and the idea of marriage, much less of having a family, scared the living daylights out of them. I am simplifying a very complex person and a complicated life for the purposes of illustration, but suffice it to say that Jody was stuck on a treadmill of falling for men who would not resemble in any way her dependent, suffocating, emotionally demanding father. Her problem was that she went too far in the other direction and hooked up with men who couldn't imagine themselves in a committed relationship or assuming the responsibility of a family. So Jody was trapped between what she thought was the ideal mate and the reality that this type of man was fundamentally unable to give her what she ultimately wanted from the relationship.

Your Past Repeats in the Present

We all hold in our heads a pattern, or a blueprint, for what it is like to be in love and in a loving relationship, based on our experiences, interpretations of our past, and our expectations of the future. As we can see with Jody's story, however, the myth that opposites attract is just that—a myth. Jody was scarred by her relationship with her father, who demanded total and unswerving attention to his needs. She saw how this impaired her mother, and she wasn't going to let that happen to her, so she left her father, determined only to be with men who wouldn't make claims on her.

Yet underneath the tough, independent Jody was another woman, someone who wanted to care for and be cared for by a family—her own family. She craved the love and attention she'd never received from her mother, and she was set on making things right, by giving the child she wanted the attention she had felt deprived of while growing up. Jody discovered that the men she was attracted to, the men who she thought were the opposite of her father, also unfortunately tended to be men who didn't want children. So Jody found herself in a double-bind. She desperately wanted a family but was attracted to men for whom the parental role was anathema.

The big surprise came later, though. In conversations with Jody, I learned that Jody's grandmother had been repeatedly spurned by her husband, Jody's grandfather. Her grandmother had tried unsuccessfully, with quite a bit of nagging and cajoling, to get her husband to give her the love she needed, to no avail. Not only did he physically abuse her, but one day when Jody's mother was a year old, her grandfather got so angry with her grandmother, for taking he without permission, that he didn't talk to his wife for three years—he literally never spoke directly to her for three entire years, as punishment! So when it came time for Jody's mother to choose her mate, she thought she was selecting someone who was the opposite of her father, a man who wouldn't be physically abusive and always irritated. Instead, however, she selected a boyfriend who was equally cruel with his relentless demand that she attend to his every whim and need. It was a relationship in which she found herself always giving but was never allowed to take any pleasure or receive attention for herself.

Now it was Jody's turn. She didn't want to choose a man who would abuse her by taking all of her love and giving back little or none, as her mother and grandmother had done. Yet the men she hooked up with were good at being boyfriends but lousy at long-term commitment. The breakthrough came when Jody realized that the men she thought were the exact opposites of her father and grandfather, all of the men she thought she was carefully choosing and pursuing, were really like them after all. They were unable to commit or share their love but were very good at extracting affection from their lovers. This was just a variation on the theme of withholding affection and refusing to truly commit.

It is uncanny how patterns of past relationships that occurred in previous generations can be reenacted and struggled with in the here and now. It's not unimaginable that the problems you are experiencing in your relationship were encountered previously by your parents and their parents before them. Having watched your parents' relationships, maybe you vowed never to be in the predicament that you unfortunately find yourself in right now. But here you are, seeking solutions for a way to break the pattern of behavior that is leaving you exhausted and deflated.

The Puzzle of Your Family's Past

This entire session will be devoted to one exercise divided into four parts. Like pieces of a puzzle that only you can solve, it's easy and fun. Quite simply, you are going to produce two types of diagrams that will depict various aspects of your family relationships. The first one is called an artwork, because it resembles a piece of modern art, with objects juxtaposed on a work surface to represent the relational ties you hold with your family. The second type of diagram is a genogram, a drawing based on the artwork, which will give you a sharper visualization of what's going on in your relationships.

Both the artwork and the genogram are loosely based on the idea of a family tree. They will depict the emotional bonds between you and the members of your family. Starting to build your artwork will be like setting off on a complex detective hunt or doing a large puzzle. It always amazes my clients that often a past dilemma that was never properly worked out in previous generations has inserted itself into the present for them to rehash over and over again. Some patterns will be obvious, as in the case of a young woman who had an abusive alcoholic father and now finds herself married to a man who ends up becoming an alcoholic after he loses his job. Other patterns will require a bit of probing and detective work before you uncover them.

Don't underestimate the power of actually doing the exercises. Reading about them will help you perform them correctly and will give you important instructions on how to properly interpret your results. But reading is a passive activity, and nothing can replace the hands-on experience of doing the exercises themselves. The physical activity provides access to information, emotions, and thoughts you've kept hidden or out of sight for a very long time.

One couple, working together with their genograms, discovered that both sets of parents had married without the approval of *their* parents. The surprise came when the couple realized the connection because they, too, had run off to get married against their parents' wishes, unsuspectingly repeating the family tradition.

EXERCISE

Part 1: Make an Artwork from Your Past Patterns

When I do this exercise with clients, I use my big collection of buttons and a wide surface, such as the kitchen table or the living room floor. The buttons will represent various members of the client's family, so it helps that I have all shapes, sizes, textures, and styles of buttons. You needn't use buttons, however; you can use any object to construct a collage, such as small stones, pebbles, coins, jelly beans, pieces of ribbon, magazine cutouts, or even an assortment of dried flowers.

Collect about fifteen to thirty objects so that you have plenty of different choices with which to describe your various relationships. It might be tempting to read ahead in this session, but be patient and follow the instructions as I lay them out, so that the revelations have the best chance to present themselves to you. And because this exercise can take up to twenty minutes, leave yourself plenty of time to engage with the activity, and work in a place where you won't be disturbed.

You are now going to make an artwork with the objects you've selected, based on the emotional bonds you felt with members of your family and significant others when you were growing up. Start by selecting an object—let's say, a button, for the purposes of this demonstration—that will represent you when you were a young girl, about six or seven years old. Put your button down in front of you, in the center of a large uncluttered surface.

Next, you will choose a button to represent, in turn, your father, mother, brothers and sisters (if you have them), aunts, uncles, cousins, and even the neighbors next door, if they played a significant role in your growing up. Place these people's buttons on the surface with the button that represents you as a child. The distance between your button and their buttons should approximate the closeness you felt toward them and how connected they were to one another. Go back as far as you can remember, and be sure to include everyone with whom you had an emotional attachment, even if they are now dead, and put them into your artwork.

For example, select a button that represents your mother. Place your mother's button at an appropriate distance from your button. Place it close to your button if you felt close to her as a child, or at a distance if you felt yourself estranged from her. Do the same with each member of your family, relatives, and any significant others. Also, remember to try to capture not only their relationship to you but their relationship to one another. If your father and mother fought all the time and didn't seem very close (but they were individually very close to you), your artwork should represent that by having their buttons on opposite sides of yours. Let your feelings guide where you put all of the buttons, and remember how you felt toward these people and how they acted toward one another.

When you feel that you have completed this artwork, stop and take a step back to look it over. What do you see? Does your "family snapshot" hold any surprises? How difficult was it to match the objects with your relatives? Was it hard to get the distances just right between your objects, especially as you added more "people" to the picture? If you did use buttons, is your dad a solid, dependable brown button? Is your sister a wild, unconventional, jagged-edged button?

• •

Open Your Notebook

This first exercise can be very emotional and cathartic. The more investment you put into it, the more insight the artwork will provide in return. Keep your notebook nearby, and as you make associations and discoveries, write them down as well as any revelations, thoughts, and difficulties you had during the exercise. Are you shocked to see how few people were in your family when you were growing up? Did you have trouble remembering your grandparents and their relationships to other people? Some of my clients discover that they were not as close to one parent as they thought they were. Others recognize sibling rivalries that they hadn't been aware of in the past. One woman never fully appreciated her aunt's influence in her life until she did the artwork. What caught you by surprise? What arrangement of buttons brought out an emotion in you?

• •

Sally and Wayne's Artwork: Adding Sally's Family

Let me now introduce you to Sally. She was a client of mine, a young woman of twenty, and when she visited my practice, it was clear that she was very fragile and vulnerable. As she spoke, her sentences trailed off into a breathless whisper. During the session, she returned time and again to a defensive posture, fastening her arms across her chest and hunching her shoulders in a way that conveyed to me that she felt the need to both protect herself and physically hold herself together. Making eye contact was difficult for Sally, and she seemed most comfortable returning her gaze to the little vase of flowers by the side of her chair. Everything about Sally's quiet and modest demeanor practically screamed: Stay away! Keep your distance!

Sally started her artwork by picking a tiny blue button from my collection to represent herself. She placed it in the center of the floor in front of her. She then picked up a big black button for her uncle and put it as far away from her button as possible. She had looked for her uncle's button first and had taken a long time to pick it out of the box. Initially, Sally did not even want to select buttons for her parents, but she finally chose a big fluffy button for her mother and placed it and the button for her mother's boyfriend far away from her button. Next, she selected buttons to represent her brother and her sister but put them near her dad, because they were much closer to him. Last, she selected both sets of grandparents who were fairly insignificant and did not play a big role in her early life. Looking at the finished artwork, I felt very sad for the little blue button all by itself on the floor, and when Sally noticed it too, she began to cry.

As her therapy progressed, I learned more about her past, and the riddle of her artwork became crystal clear. Sally had been sexually abused by her uncle at the age of four and again when she was ten. After that, she was sent away to live for a while in foster care.

It was a powerful and very dramatic story. I tell you Sally's story, however, fully aware that your story—and your artwork—will be very different. I selected Sally because it is an extreme situation (although you may be surprised at how many women share aspects of her story!), and I think it will give you a better idea of how the exercise works. But everyone's story is unique, so don't let the specifics of her situation get in the way of exploring your own story and creating your own artwork. Sally's tale and how she performed the exercise are not intended to be an exact model or even a template. I offer them because I think that describing how another person experiences the exercise is terribly instructive, but don't be constrained by Sally's example or any preconceived idea of how your artwork should look. Move the buttons around, feeling, as it were, for the right juxtaposition that represents each one's relationship to your button and all of the other buttons in your artwork. Yes, you'll actually feel it when the button is moved into the right position.

EXERCISE

Part 2: Make an Artwork from Your Present Patterns

In the next phase of this exercise, I want you to repeat the previous exercise, but now change your artwork to show the relationships in your life as they are today. Have the buttons that used to be so close to your button in the past drifted off? Who has died? Or, maybe, over time, you have become closer to your siblings and they now occupy a space nearer to your button?

Change your artwork by assigning buttons and positions to everyone who is significant in your life right now, in the present. Choose buttons or other objects for all of the new people in your life at this moment in time, as the adult you are now, and place them at a distance according to the same rules as in the previous artwork. Their positions should reflect the strength of their emotional bonds to you and to one another in the present moment.

If you feel differently now than you did when you were a child about a member of your family, feel free to swap objects so that it represents a closer approximation of how you feel now. Spend no more than ten minutes constructing your Present Patterns artwork.

It's going to be tricky, I grant you. It will probably take more than one or two tries to get it right. But if you test the position for each button as you would test a piece of a jigsaw puzzle to see whether it fits properly, you'll find that with a bit of patience, everything will come together quite nicely.

Sally and Wayne's Artwork: Adding Wayne's Family

Let's return to Sally's artwork and how it changed when she added Wayne's family.

She first selected two of the sunniest, shiniest buttons to represent her two young children and placed them right next to her button. Then she put Wayne's button (quite a big black one!) and his parents very close to one another but on the other side of her and her children. There was also a large gap between Sally and Wayne, obviously signifying the rift they were experiencing at the time.

Next, she selected a button for Wayne's sister-in-law and placed it very close to Wayne, because Sally suspected that she was sleeping with Wayne. She put Wayne's brother's button far away from everyone.

Observe Your Artwork

When you've finished your artwork, take a moment to reflect on what you see before you. It might seem silly, but look at your artwork to see whether you've remembered to include your partner. Strange as it may seem, about 40 percent of my clients forget to put their men in the second phase! They add the kids, their mother- and father-in-law, even their partner's best friend, but forget to actually put their boyfriend or husband into the artwork. If you have forgotten him, it will provide food for thought. Is he insignificant in your life, meaningless? Does he have no say? No power? Do you really wish he would go away? Maybe you feel very separate about your family and his, and they simply don't blend. Write down in your notebook some thoughts about how this revelation makes you feel and what you think might be the reason that he is the last thing on your mind when you look at your present life. If you have put him in the artwork, what does he look like? Why did you pick that object for him? Briefly jot it all down.

Be the Therapist: A Time for Reflection

If you used buttons for these exercises, what kind did you choose for each person? Did you select a frilly button for a prissy sister? A green one for a jealous sister? A cracked one for an abusive grandfather?

Also pay close attention to where you placed the buttons in relation to the button that represents you. Perhaps you put one of your siblings on one side of your button and your other sibling's button on the other side, because they never did get along and you were always playing the role of intermediary. If your boyfriend's mother is emotionally very close to him but not to you, did your artwork show this by the placement of his mother's button touching the far side of his button? Maybe you positioned your boyfriend's mother midway between your button and his and off to one side, because his mother often gets between the two of you. How does that make you feel? If you get along with his sister better than he does, did you put her button closer to your button than to his? What about his father? Where does he fit into the picture? What about his ex, whom he sees occasionally just as a friend? What about his child, who comes to stay with you on the weekends? Did you select a button for each member of his family and relatives, and how hard was it to blend his family with yours?

If you have children, did you include them? Where does your son and/or daughter fit into your button constellation? Is your daughter touching your button and your son touching your partner's? If you have ex-husbands or ex-boyfriends and they are actively in your life, did you put them into your artwork? If not, why not? If your daughter is spending more time with your ex-husband/her dad, did you find a way to portray that relationship in your artwork?

Make notes in your notebook about the emotional impact the exercise had on you. Remember, nothing is right and nothing is wrong. You don't have to write in complete sentences. Simple phrases or even a single word will do just fine. Capture your feelings as best you can, so that you can remember your revelations and use them later. If you have a camera or a cell phone handy, take a quick photo of your artwork so that you can refer to it later.

What Is Your Artwork Telling You about Your Family History?

Over the years, I have seen how powerful the artwork can be in presenting a quick, revealing, and dramatic snapshot of a person's interrelationships. I have many examples of how this exercise can provide a rich source of material for my clients to work from. I recall a woman from my practice named Sarah, who used matching buttons for herself, her three sisters, and her mother. Later, when she put down her husband's button, she picked a little green one. She picked the same green buttons for all three of her sister's husbands, too! It turned out that all of the husbands were farmers. As she told me her stories, she kept getting confused about who was who in her artwork, and she realized that she also confused them in real life. Her dad was a factory worker and was very different from the husbands she and her sisters had chosen. Her father was represented by a black button. She explained that she had never felt special when she was little; she never stood out and felt that no one took any notice of her. It became apparent to Sarah, looking at all of her buttons, how she had felt growing up.

Another woman, who was doing this exercise in my office—I'll call her Ellie—took a very long time in selecting a button for her husband and then began to talk to the button as if it were her spouse, although he was sitting right beside her. She clutched the button between her fingers close to her face and started to sob. She told him (the button) how much she loved him and was so sorry she hadn't been there for him when his father died recently. It was a remarkable and cathartic moment.

Once a young lady I helped in my therapy practice simply scooped up a handful of buttons and dumped them on top of her first artwork, which had consisted only of herself and her family. When I asked her what was happening, she said that the pile of buttons was her husband's family. There were at least fifty buttons all piled on top of her and her husband! Clearly, his large family was burying their relationship. Another young woman actually took a button and threw it across the room, smashing it in two. There are so many rich stories and small details to be gleaned from the artwork. So, take your time to explore yourself and your relationships through this exercise, and remember to jot down in your notebook the emotions, revelations, and connections that occur to you.

If you are patient and honest, I'm sure that you now see aspects of your interpersonal relationships in a new light. Maybe you realize how intrusive your boyfriend's siblings are when you try to spend more time with him? Perhaps you see clearly how completely cut off you are from your own family, having substituted his for yours for the sake of the relationship?

We will return to your artwork for the last part of this exercise, so tape down the buttons or the objects you are using and keep the artwork in a safe place, or photograph it so that you can reconstruct it later.

You have now completed the first two phases of the exercise, both of which involve the construction of a three-dimensional representation of your past and present relationships. As confident as

I am that these artworks have given you a new perspective on your relationships, I am equally sure that the next two exercises will provoke further revelations on your journey of self-discovery. Believe me, things are going to get even more interesting.

Remember when I mentioned that the first step in gaining control of your relationship and your partner is to liberate yourself from the hurtful and counterproductive influences in your past? These echoes contain the messages that condemn you to make the same bad choices and repeat the same self-destructive behavior over and over again. Well, you are now ready to take the next step and make those patterns even more recognizable and therefore correctable.

Your Genogram

I am going to take the idea of the artwork to the next level by teaching you how to draw a genogram. *Genogram* is just a fancy word taken from the Latin *gen*, meaning "one that is produced," and *gram*, meaning "something that is written or drawn." So a rough translation is that a genogram is a picture that portrays how you were produced. A genogram, in therapeutic terms, is a diagram of the people and the forces in your past and present that are responsible for shaping your emotional self. It's a snapshot of who you are and how you came to be that way.

Many predictable patterns of conflict will be revealed when you draw your genogram. The themes, myths, issues, and behaviors that originate in your past and that cause problems in your present relationship will be brought to the surface for you to recognize and analyze. This exercise will be a blueprint of both your family system and his, joined together in one diagram. You will be able to read this relational road map to help you discover the repeating patterns of both of your families' generations.

At first, as you go about filling in your genogram in your notebook, it will resemble a traditional family tree. It will have symbols for your relatives, their ages, connections to whomever they married, how many children they had, and so on. But there the similarities end, because it will contain a lot more information than a traditional family tree does, information that will help you better understand those patterns I've been discussing, the ones that are the source of conflict in your relationships.

Your genogram will be constructed from two layers of information:

1. The basics: Like a family tree, the first layer of information consists of the names, ages, occupations, marriages, and deaths of your family members.

2. Personal characteristics: This second layer of information contains brief descriptions of each person's family label or role (comic, diplomat, caregiver, host). Basically, you'll jot down any traits that you think are significant (for example, alcoholic, went to prison, abuser, married five times).

Many of these details you already know; however, some of the information will require you to ask questions in order to get the answers you need. For example, family backgrounds tend to be obscured by lore and legend, and often certain incidents have been buried or unspoken about for many years.

I don't intend for you to stir up a hornets' nest of trouble in your family. You'll need to tread carefully and gently to obtain the information without causing unnecessary irritation or anger. Questions about circumstances in relatives' lives can be emotionally charged because they involve difficult topics such as alcoholism, abuse, stillbirth, adoption, and suicide. You may not know that when your parents divorced, it was the same year that your mom's mother died unexpectedly from a heart attack, or that your cousin is the child resulting from your aunt's affair with another man who isn't your uncle.

Remember that information is power. With each bit of information you are able to include in your genogram, connections can be made that will reveal the patterns that echo through your emotional life.

EXERCISE

Part 3: Drawing Your Genogram

You have done the groundwork and are now ready to draw your genogram.

Start by drawing a medium-size circle near the bottom right-hand corner of the page; write your name and age inside the circle, with your occupation just above it. Next, draw a medium-size square near the bottom left-hand corner of the paper, write your partner's name and age inside the square, and, just above his name, put his occupation. Next, draw a long horizontal line connecting the two shapes. If you are married, draw a double line; if you are in a committed relationship, draw a single line. Above the line, write down the number of years you both have been together. If you have children, add them beneath the line, with their names and ages. Finally, add your relatives and his relatives to complete the genogram. Your genograms will also include these people's names. The three genograms on page 57 are shown as examples to help you create your own.

Don't worry if you don't know a lot about his side of the family. You can ask him the next time you are relaxing together, thereby providing you with another opportunity to practice actively listening to him, as you did in session 1. You will be able to fill out his side of the genogram without his realizing what you are up to and with the added benefit of showing him that you are interested in his life and family.

You'll need several sheets of scrap paper, because you will likely go through a few drafts in order to get the spacing and the juxtaposition of all of your relatives appropriately placed on the page. It's a good idea to use a pencil. And, again, take your time to engage with the exercise, instead of just rushing through it. Don't worry if you don't have all of the information at your fingertips to complete your genogram. First and foremost, get everything that you do know down on paper; you can identify any gaps and fill them in later.

This first genogram depicts a couple, in which the two people have been married seven years.

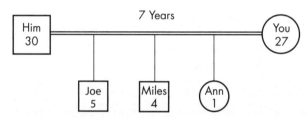

The couple's children are added to the genogram.

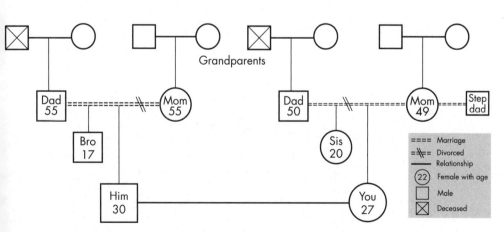

In this final genogram, the couple's relatives are added.

Make the Connections

You are now ready to add the information layer to your diagram.

Summarize in a brief phrase or a descriptive word or two each of the standout features or qualities of every relative and write it down above, in, or across the circle or the square that represents this person. If what you remember was that his or her standout characteristic was being abusive, an alcoholic, a drifter, religious, a workaholic, an orphan, or a womanizer, be sure to write that down. If some relatives were of a different nationality or religion, note it on your genogram. If anyone was the family caregiver or had multiple marriages, write that on your genogram. If there was a cousin who went to jail or certain relatives had trouble with the law, add that to your genogram. Trust that your first impression and recollection of the person will have the most meaning for this exercise. If necessary, invent your own symbols or abbreviations. Customize the genogram to make it your own.

Again, if you have a large family, your genogram will look a bit crowded and messy. Your genogram is for you alone, and no one will see it unless you permit it. But in order for you to recognize recurring patterns, it is important to keep it as neat and clear as possible. Doing your artworks has prepared you to get the most from your genogram. All that you are really doing is putting it into map form.

Now step back and look at your genogram. Draw circles, preferably with colored pens or pencils, around the people on your genogram who have the same issues, whether it be a conflict with their parents, rivalry with siblings, or intense closeness with women family members but lukewarm relations with the men. Let yourself simply take in the genogram with all of the descriptions. If you've taken the time and done the exercise carefully and used the revelations and the connections from your artwork, I guarantee that patterns will soon emerge, patterns you will quickly recognize are repeating themselves in your own life.

For example, maybe you have clearly depicted that your partner's family has a habit of always blaming you for his problems.

In creating the genogram, however, you see that his family has idolized the sons and blamed the daughters-in-law going back two generations. Perhaps there are a few "only sons" on your boyfriend's generation's side who never seemed to be financially or emotionally independent enough to strike out on their own or have jobs or families. In your genogram, you may see how your partner's grown son, who is living at home and accepts an allowance from his father, is repeating that same pattern. Or maybe your boyfriend's brother is the favorite, the golden boy who can do no wrong, and when you closely look at your genogram, you realize that he bears an uncanny resemblance to his father's brother, who was also the favorite in the family, with your guy's father being considered the "loser." Does this ring any bells?

At this point, you'll need to apply yourself to the exercise because, as with a puzzle, you are hunting for similarities that connect people to people and groups to groups. When you find them, remember to draw a circle around them to remind yourself that they are connected. Everyone's genogram is different, but the patterns are there. Look for recurring themes, issues, and myths that may have been repeated in your families. You may have the theme of alcoholism or drugs running through your family or perhaps all of the men were in law enforcement, transportation, medicine, or sales. There might be a strong current of divorce running through your genogram. Family feuds. Jealousies. Abandonment. Whatever the patterns, hunt them out.

When you think you are finished, I'd like you to take a fresh look at your genogram and really try hard to see whether you have forgotten a very significant person or maybe someone whom no one notices or ever talks about. One of my clients forgot to put her father's second wife of fifteen years into her genogram! Another forgot to add her stepsister, although she actually felt very close to her. We often have blind spots when thinking about our families. It is sometimes an eye-opener to notice the people whom you forget to add to your diagram. Jot it all down in your notebook.

Connect Your Past Family Themes

Working with your genogram's patterns, you will start to link conflicts that are in your current relationship with those that have also caused trouble in the relationships of your past and present relatives. Trust me! In my private practice over the years, I have used this exercise countless times to reveal the emotional connections between a couple's past and present families. It is merely a tool, but it will give you immediate insights into your family issues that you may not have recognized previously. You will probably be startled to see a repetitive theme or a charged issue literally pop up from your notebook as you write down your thoughts and impressions.

And remember, take your time with this exercise and try to be instinctive; let your first choices be the ones you stick with. It is often difficult to see your family this way, even if you are already familiar with the problems and the themes. The genogram always provides a different and illuminating perspective.

For the last part of this exercise, I think it's time for you to have a little fun. You've worked hard at uncovering some troubling and probably painful patterns, so now you can sit back and give yourself a break. You deserve it! We're going to leave behind the problems and complexities of your real world and, for a moment, step into a fantasy world of your own making. One in which the relationships are comfortable, intimate, rewarding. A world in which your man is attentive and responds to your needs and desires. A world in which you are able to control the communication between you and your lover and you receive the appreciation and the affection you've been missing.

EXERCISE

Part 4: Your Fantasy Future

At this point, I'd like you to go back to your artwork and carefully remove the tape holding down your buttons or objects to the paper, or else re-create the artwork using your photo to guide you.

Now begin to reposition the buttons, the jelly beans, or whatever objects you are using, and let them reflect the kind of relationship you have only dared to fantasize about. Don't be hampered by what is; simply let yourself be guided entirely by what would make you truly happy. Here is a chance to end the conflict and create a life you have dreamed of. Express your secret desires in your artwork. Have you been thinking about taking a lover? About being with other guys? Maybe you fantasize about banishing your domineering mother from your life? Do you want loads of children? Would you like to be closer to a friend of whom your man disapproves? Perhaps you want to play with moving your partner on and off the artwork to see what it feels like to break up with him? Take your deepest desires out of the closet and express them through the artwork. Move your buttons freely. Remove the buttons of people with whom you no longer want to associate.

Realizing Your Goals

You are not merely giving free rein to the desires you've kept under lock and key all of these years. You are also taking an important step in the course of your journey. You are setting a destination for where you want to be at the end of this book. Therapists call this "goal setting," and it is an important act to enable you to achieve success in your relationship, so that you truly end up where you want to go.

Often my clients' Fantasy Future artworks are actually very doable and are not fantastic or unattainable. But yours can be as far-fetched as you like. It can really be helpful to overreach in your dreams and fantasies, in order to be able to settle realistically for something that is later obtainable—which is not to say that you can't start over entirely if you want. One client scooped up all of the buttons and started again with a whole new set of buttons to build a very different Fantasy Future artwork.

Another woman replaced all of the men with big leather buttons, her idea of the perfect man. Another got rid of all of her family buttons completely, added five buttons representing their children, and grouped her husband's family around just her, her husband, and their children.

The variations are endless, but the Fantasy Future artwork is unique and totally yours.

Of course, it is impossible to bring back to life loved ones who have died, just as it is probably equally unrealistic to repair some very damaged relationships. But I want this Fantasy Future artwork to serve as a general plan of attack, if you will, a way to approach your future. Perhaps you can work on getting to know your guy's parents better, as a way to break a pattern of jealous control. Or you can mend the rift between you and your sister, to change the repeating pattern of hostility between the women members of your family that stretches back more than a hundred years. By setting goals, you will also have highlighted certain boundaries as a couple and identified whom you are letting get too close and whom you'd like to come nearer. As a final list in your notebook, write down what your Fantasy Future artwork helped you realize and what you need to think about to ensure the changes you want in the future.

Understanding = Choice

You have come a long way in a short time and have accomplished a great deal in this session. You should be justifiably proud of yourself. And so, award yourself the second gift from the list you compiled earlier and wrote down in your notebook. This gift to yourself symbolizes a session badge that represents Making Connections. You deserve it. The path you have followed has shown you how your past is connected to your future, and now you have the necessary awareness to break undesirable patterns that do not give you what you want in your relationship. You have revealed the repetitive behavior and choices that destined you to repeat the same mistakes over and over again.

Are you ready to break the mold? To possess the knowledge of why you reenact age-old interpersonal conflicts in your own life? To take control of the relationship and discover why you are with your man? The key to achieving your own unique brand of intimacy in your relationship awaits you in the next session.

Why Are You with Him?

Have you noticed that you can usually walk into a crowded bar or party and instantly spot the hot guy? Your antennae start to tingle practically before you even exchange glances with him across the room. You are picking up on an indescribable but very definite vibe—something's telling you he is your "guy type." It happens in a nanosecond. And your next thought is, Mmm, think I'll check him out. You don't even notice that an equally delicious mmm is sitting right next to him.

"Being attracted" to someone is a phrase that describes the experience perfectly. On an emotional level, it can feel like a kind of erotic curiosity, a vague awareness of being interested, or an urge to get to know a man a bit better. It's not only his eyes or his smile or his body, exactly—although these things are a big turn-on. Something you can't quite put into words draws you toward him and compels you to give it a try.

It all sounds so romantic, so dreamy and out of this world. After all of my years of helping women in their relationships, I still believe in love at first sight, but probably not in the same way that you do. I'm sorry if I am stepping on a cherished notion of yours, but one of the core concepts in my couples practice is that the reason adults get together in a romantic relationship is to rework unresolved issues from their childhood. This is something you've now experienced from doing your genogram in session 2. Women (and men) instinctively recognize the person who will lead them into the repetitive patterns of past generations, who will enable them to relive conflicts and fears from past family difficulties and disappointments. All of the dynamics you so diligently unearthed in the last session were actually at work while you were busy falling in love.

I'd like to start this session by asking you to think about the qualities that first attracted you to your partner. The man who began the relationship so perfectly but soon began to disappoint, sadden, anger, and even hurt you. We will return to this very important turning point, but for now, try to remember what it was like in the early days. What were the things he said that made you laugh? The quirky little things that endeared him to you? Was it the way he touched you or seemed so attentive?

What I'm asking of you might be difficult and painful. These memories may bring to the surface feelings of bitterness, of having been duped and deceived and left high and dry. But believe me, thinking about what first attracted you to your partner is a key that will unlock many secrets about your dissolving relationship and cycle of bad choices in boyfriends. This is an essential step you'll take to bring about positive change in yourself, your man, and your relationship.

In practical terms, this will help you develop your own personal "lens" to bring into sharp focus the hidden forces that attracted you to your partner and will help you see what lies under the surface that is causing problems in your relationship. Think of it as manufacturing your own special pair of eyeglasses, enabling you to see the inner mechanism of your relationship, so that you can make it work better. Yet an even bigger surprise lies ahead as you construct this lens: once you see the hidden needs and feelings that drew you to your mate, you will also know the hidden needs that attracted him to you—because they are similar. This secret knowledge will provide you with a powerful mechanism with which to steer the relationship.

Let's dig deeper and begin to construct your relationship lens by thinking of how you felt about your boyfriend in the early days. What are some of the more obvious reasons for your attraction that come to mind? Was it the way he handled himself among his friends? Was it his sense of humor or his athletic good looks? Maybe it was the way he was so polite and considerate on your first date? These are very real and valid reasons why you chose the man you did, but they are only the tip of the iceberg, the part that is exposed above the surface and perceptible in the sunlight of your everyday awareness.

Delving into Your Psychic Closet

Let me introduce you to a woman I helped recently—I'll call her Anna—whom I will use to illustrate the process of creating your relationship lens.

Anna presented herself as superorganized and in control. She arranged her coat, purse, cell phone, and diary on the small table next to her chair, on her lap, and on the floor by her feet, giving the impression that she needed to know exactly where her possessions were at any given moment to quickly get her hands on them. I usually begin the first session with a client by asking what brings her to therapy. But in Anna's case, she first wanted to have a discussion about what I would call "housekeeping" details. For example, exactly how long were the therapy sessions, if she came early could she sit in the office's waiting room, how might she contact me if she found herself running late? As she told her story, the reason for Anna's attention to practical detail became clear.

Anna had lost her mother at a very early age. Her father had to work long, hard hours in a supermarket to keep the family financially afloat. Because Anna was the eldest of three siblings, it fell to her to take care of the house. She spent her teenage years and her early twenties looking after the family, keeping the refrigerator stocked and making meals, balancing the weekly budget, doing the laundry, and monitoring the schedules of her two brothers and her father.

As she got older, Anna found herself in relationships with men who always seemed to be in a mess. Whether her man was drifting from job to job, repeatedly short of cash for cigarettes, groceries, or beer, or simply showing up late all of the time, Anna knew how to close the gap, keep him on track, and provide the emotional support her needy boyfriend demanded of her.

After about six months, however, she began to feel burdened and bored. She told me that it was time she got something out of the relationship for herself. That's when she accidentally discovered that her boyfriend was cheating on her. She confronted him with a photograph he had carelessly left on his cell phone, but he said all of the right things, acted helpless and repentant, and convinced her that he'd change. Of course, he didn't. And three months after that, she was back at square one with him: miserable and burdened but unable to break it off.

After diligent work in therapy, Anna came to realize that she had been attracted to her boyfriend's excessive neediness. On some level, it was a relationship that felt familiar, a role she knew how to play in exchange for feeling useful and needed. That's because at the relationship's core, she was reliving the role she had been cast in as a result of her mother's death. Anything she attempted to do to change it felt like a betrayal, not only of her father and brothers, but also of her dead mother's memory. Anna realized that she had selected the type of man who would help her fulfill the role she had been trained for, and accustomed to, from an early age. Once she saw this, she was able to quickly move beyond the limits of her old behavior to renew a desire for a more balanced and deeper intimacy with her partner. Armed with this understanding and strengthened by her new self-awareness, she began a regimen of exercises similar to those found in this book and was able to steer the relationship—and her man—to a new, more satisfying and loving experience.

It was hard work for Anna, and it will probably be difficult in the beginning for you as well. It was certainly uncomfortable for her, to say the least. But that's how it should be. And once you work through it, the rewards are abundant and the possibility of having a loving long-term relationship is more realistic and attainable than ever.

EXERCISE

Couple Fit—Your Blueprint

Your assignment for this week is to shine a light into the dark recesses of your unconscious and recognize the true reasons you are in your relationship by compiling several lists. I call this exercise "Couple Fit," and it is a core concept of my therapy technique. The Couple Fit will help you understand the hidden dynamics that made you select your partner. Once the purpose behind your choice is revealed, your relationship problems will be much easier for you to understand and retool.

Understand, Act, and Change

Typically, I am able to guide couples to realize helpful insights in the first few sessions. There are, however, certain approaches to couples therapy that use techniques that require months, if not years, to produce results. I'm simply not into a slow, plodding, dawdling process of analysis. I prefer rapid but deep and lasting results. In my private practice, the average course of therapy is ten sessions. Just by being "in relationship" with each other, a couple can continue to use the understandings and insights they gain during their sixty-minute sessions to work out their conflicts on their own.

You'll need your notebook to create the lists that I'll discuss a little later in the session. The first list will be five things that attracted you to your man when you first met him. The second list will be five things that make you dissatisfied with the relationship now. These likes and dislikes should be obvious to you, and the wording needn't be particularly deep or clever. By writing these lists quickly and honestly, you can use them to glimpse what is going on behind the closed door of your psyche's inner closet. I have used this exercise in my practice hundreds of times to help women fit together the puzzle pieces of their relationships.

Let's see how Anna completed this list. Here are the five things that attracted her to Jim.

List A

1. He was quiet but still had a carefree, happy-go-lucky attitude about life, never letting anything worry him or get him down.

2. Had the sweetest puppy-dog smile, his hair always a bit messy, and his shirts were always two sizes too big.

3. Was always so appreciative and complimentary when I did things like take him shopping or fix him spaghetti.

4. So easy to be with, I didn't have to try to be funny or entertaining. Just hanging out in the evening, drinking wine and beer, reading magazines and watching TV until it was time for bed.

5. I think it turned him on when I initiated sex.

Your Pro and Con Lists

In your notebook write down five things that first attracted you to your man (List A). Remember, Anna did not take long to complete this list. She didn't think twice about it, and neither should you.

I can't emphasize this too strongly: simply let the ideas pop into your head. Don't doubt or second-guess yourself. There are no wrong responses. Trust the first thoughts that come into your mind.

Remember: if you spend more than fifteen minutes doing this, you are trying too hard. Go on! Put the book down, write your list, and come back when you're done.

Now, on a clean page, write down the five things that really piss you off about your boyfriend and the relationship (List B). Don't hold back. Don't try to be fair or go easy on him. You've been carrying the anger and hurt around inside long enough to be able to tell it like it is.

Here's Anna's list of the five things that made her unhappy in her relationship.

List B

1. I wish he would chase after me in the bedroom once in a while.

2. He's lazy, pure and simple. Does the absolute minimum when it comes to taking care of things, including himself!

3. Expects me to do everything for him.

4. Never shows any real passion for anything other than beer, baseball, and his buddies.

5. I can't have a social life. He always wants me to stay home with him and sulks for two days if I go out with my friends for a couple of hours.

The Love/Hate Enigma That Draws You to Your Man

The next step is to review the two lists and look for connections or similarities. I know what you're probably saying: "Weren't the two lists supposed to be totally opposite?" But the fact is, the very qualities that attract you to someone may be the same things that, with a slight twist, can also make you wish you'd never met the man.

Let me show you what I mean. Let's quickly review Anna's two lists. In her first list, she described the things that attracted her to Jim as a man who was quiet and carefree, totally even-tempered. He appreciated the ways she took care of him, and he was someone with whom she could see herself spending quiet time. Last, and certainly not least, Jim let her take charge in bed.

Now let's look at her second list: the things about her man that made her so unhappy. The man whom she used to enjoy caring for is now someone who she wishes would take responsibility for the way he looks, as well as help maintain order in the house. The attachment that masqueraded as intimacy has become so suffocating that she can't even form relationships outside of the couple. Her fondness for his even temper has turned into a longing for him to get excited and express real, even wild, emotions about something—anything—other than his boring habits and friends. Sex has become predictable, and she wishes that he'd show some passion, instead of being the passive one between the sheets.

See what I mean? Sometimes what first attracted you to your man has gone terribly wrong and now is a turnoff. It is something of a cliché, I know, that attraction and repulsion are two sides of the same coin. When you see it play out in your life, however, the revelation can pack quite a punch.

Pinpointing the Pain

Now, look over your two lists. Have aspects of his personality that you once found so attractive and mentioned in List A morphed into the qualities in List B that you now find disappointing or that cause conflict? You might have been attracted to your guy because he was so lively and outgoing; now he is simply a loudmouth, going out all the time, surrounding himself with a crowd of admirers so that he can be the life of the party. Was he such a good listener in the beginning, interested in the details of your day and nodding along as you openly and freely expressed your feelings, yet now you find out that he is really withdrawn and never truly talks about what he's thinking or feeling, and it was all a clever dodge to avoid any real interaction? Or maybe you admired his vitality, his totally hot physique, and how he seemed so well put together, yet you've discovered after these many months that he spends more time on the free weights at the gym than with you, he eyes himself out in the mirror more often than he checks you out, and he works harder on getting his hair just right than you do!

Let's return to your lists. When you notice two opposite but connected behaviors, put an asterisk next to them. For example, your boyfriend's casual, laid-back attitude (from List A) could be connected to his tendency to procrastinate (from List B). Well done! You are definitely on your way. Each connection you made is a gateway to begin healing your relationship right now. These insights will lead you back to painful situations and emotional discomforts that you endured in your past, which may play an important role in your present relationship. Identifying these connections will help you pinpoint the past pain that you may now be reliving.

Let's see what Anna marked with an asterisk(*) on her two lists.

(The superscript numbers at the end of each item in List A correspond to the superscript numbers in List B.)

List A

1. He was quiet but still had a carefree, happy-go-lucky attitude about life, never letting anything worry him or get him down.

2. Had the sweetest puppy-dog smile, his hair always a bit messy, and his shirts were always two sizes too big.

3. Was always so appreciative and complimentary when I did things like take him shopping or fix him spaghetti.*[1]

4. So easy to be with, I didn't have to try to be funny or enter-taining. Just hanging out in the evening, drinking wine and beer, reading magazines and watching TV until it was time for bed.[*2]

5. I think it turned him on when I initiated sex.[*3]

List B

1. I wish he would chase after me in the bedroom once in a while.[*3]

2. He's lazy, pure and simple. Does the absolute minimum when it comes to taking care of things, including himself![*1]

3. Expects me to do everything for him.

4. Never shows any real passion for anything other than beer, baseball, and his buddies.[*2]

5. I can't have a social life. He always wants me to stay home with him and sulks for two days if I go out with my friends for a couple of hours.[*2]

Now, go back to the items you marked with an asterisk in List B. Underneath this list, start a third list and call it List B's Bad Feelings. In this list, briefly describe how those particular behaviors of your guy make you feel. Do you feel *left out* because he always chooses to hang out with his friends instead of you on the weekends? Does it make you feel *isolated* when he decides to rewire the lamp he promised to fix months ago, at the very moment you try to have a serious conversation with him about the relationship? Do you feel *empty* when he does something really nice for you, like taking you to dinner or buying you flowers, because you know he feels guilty for some bad behavior you'll find out about in a couple of days or weeks? Or do you feel *rejected* when he stays up all night playing a computer game instead of coming to bed and paying attention to you? Try to connect to the feelings you have underneath your anger and frustration.

Links to Your Past

Now I'll ask you to create a fourth and final list. This time I'd like you to think back to your childhood and recall three incidents that upset you emotionally. They could be events that caused you to feel lonely, frightened, sad, or angry. Once you have picked the most prominent memories and associated them with how they make you feel, jot them down in your notebook. This is your list of Bad Childhood Emotions. These are echoes from your past that are influencing the relationship in the present. They could be feelings you experienced with your family when you were very young, or they may be related to your friends or how you were treated at school or by an authority figure in your life. The memories won't be very difficult to bring to mind; they are the ones that stay with you and still feel quite sensitive.

When Anna made this list, she placed the night her mom died right at the top. Next to it, she wrote down three words: Lonely. Afraid. Hurt. She also remembered having to iron her father's shirt, shine his shoes, and set out his clothes on the chair beside his bed for the next day. Next to that item, she wrote that she felt: Angry. Resentful. Oppressed.

Your list may contain similar memories of a time when your mother or father was gravely ill, went to the hospital, or died. You may remember instances when your family didn't have enough money and you had to wear hand-me-downs, rather than new clothing. It could be the feeling of seeing your mother or father cry for the first time or having to move away from your friends and classmates. Maybe it was the time you hurt yourself accidentally in the playground, and no one noticed or came to help you. Or the feelings you had watching your mother and father always screaming at each other. Every person's life has these little or big moments when they felt inadequate, afraid, lonely, abandoned, powerless, and intimidated. It's important to be honest with yourself and really own this list.

Review Your Emotions

Now review List B's Bad Feelings and Bad Childhood Emotions. Put a number sign (#) next to the items that contain *similar feelings* and emotions that are found in both lists. Here's a selection of what Anna's lists looked like. (The superscript numbers at the end of each item in List A correspond to the superscript numbers in List B.)

List B's Bad Feelings

I don't feel that he really appreciates me

I feel as if I am the mother, it's all down to me![1]

I am not noticed.

All alone.[2]

I am unattractive.

Bad Childhood Emotions

1. The day my mom died, I thought my whole life was ending. I have never felt so alone. Lonely. Afraid. Hurt.[2]

2. After my mother died, I hated having to set out my father's clothes on the chair beside his bed for the next day. I felt like I was being picked on unfairly. I had enough to do around the house just growing up, without having to iron his shirt and shine his shoes. Angry. Resentful. Oppressed.[1]

3. I had to bake my brothers' birthday cakes and plan their parties. But I had to plan my own birthdays myself. They couldn't be bothered.

The feelings marked with a number sign were the ones that caused conflict in Anna's relationship. They had their roots in her past but were being relived in her current relationship. Her destiny was to pick a boyfriend like Jim. He was very good at being aloof, withdrawn, and unavailable to Anna. He was also good at making Anna feel cast aside, unimportant, and ignored, which is exactly the way her father made her feel. So, you see, past hurts and scenarios keep playing themselves out in one form or another in our present relationships because they have never been resolved. Many of the women I see in therapy find themselves trapped in situations that keep repeating and repeating because they haven't come to terms with their earlier emotional distress.

Your Psychic Closet Door Opens

Look at the feelings you have marked off with a number sign (#). You may have been unaware that these early disturbing emotions were causing your relationship trouble, because they are usually hidden from your awareness, as they work secretly to destroy your possibility of having a calm, happy partnership.

We often say that opposites attract, but, in fact, guys and girls are attracted to each other if they have similar backgrounds and thus much of the same stuff in their "psychic closets."

It never ceases to amaze me to watch the couples I treat in therapy start off telling me about how they saw only the qualities that they admired in each other (List A). Oh, they were made for each other and were head over heels in love! Yet hidden from their view were the dark, frightening, horrible feelings they had firmly under lock and key in their psychic closets. The surprise here is that each partner harbors a similar emotional pain originating in his or her personal childhood environment, whether it be loss, abandonment, rejection, humiliation, or helplessness. Furthermore, over the years, each of us has developed an intuition about those we are attracted to, an unconscious awareness of their vulnerabilities, the hidden feelings they would have written down and put a number sign beside, if they had undertaken this exercise. Amazingly, then, both partners carry identical keys to activate their own old wounds and the other person's or to open the doors to each other's psychic closets, because their closets are actually the same.

You can glimpse the bad feelings and the wounds behind the door of your partner's psychic closet, because this door can never be completely shut all the time. That peek inside his psychic closet causes you to feel the chemistry or the attachment that accompanies falling in love. Over time, however, you both cannot keep your doors shut tightly enough, and the hidden feelings soon burst through, triggering the conflict you are probably experiencing now. The result is that now your guy doesn't seem like the same person you got together with at the start of the relationship.

Part of your task is to learn to open your psychic door at will and try to become more comfortable with what is behind it. As you do this, your man will have to follow suit, because, remember, what is behind your door is also behind his. What was the elephant in the room now becomes recognized and accepted by both of you as your shared issue.

Your Lens Sentence

You are now close to being able to write your "lens sentence," which will give you a lens to use throughout this book. Your lens sentence will bring into focus the conflicts in your relationship and help you identify, challenge, and change your behavior and thus change your partner's behavior. Understanding yourself will give you the key not only to your psychic closet door, but also to his. The goal of this program is not to smash down the door, but to oil the hinges and make the door very easy to swing open and shut at will.

The first section of this book has been the hardest, but once you have written your lens sentence, it will be a relationship tool you can use for the rest of your life. It is going to be your relationship blueprint.

Here I'd like you to refer back to the last two lists you've created in this session, List B's Bad Feelings and Childhood's Bad Emotions. Note the sentences or the phrases marked with number signs. These are the items that contain references to your relationship's vulnerabilities. Reflect on them for a moment. Can you identify a connecting theme that binds them? Are there any overarching emotions common to all of them? Find a word or a phrase that captures the essence of these feelings, and write it in your notebook.

The final step is to simply rearrange your word or phrase in the form of a sentence, beginning with "I am . . . " One of my clients jotted down such phrases as "left out," "pushed away," and "frightened." When she stepped back and reviewed these items, she felt that the word that best expressed these feelings was "excluded." It was now a simple matter for her to take that observation and express it as the sentence "I am afraid of being excluded." That was her lens sentence.

Another client reviewed her items marked with a number sign, which contained the phrases "felt dumb," "disappointed my family," and "screwing up." She knew right away that the common sentiment connecting these phrases was encapsulated by the word "unlovable." She quickly translated it into her lens sentence and wrote in her notebook, "I am unlovable."

For Anna, as she reviewed the items with number signs on her lists, she selected "isolated," "lonely," and "angry." The word she hit upon that seemed to say in a nutshell what she was feeling was "abandoned." Her evaluation was spot on. In Anna's case, her anger at being made to feel all alone produced feelings of abandonment. The lens sentence she wrote in her notebook was, "I am afraid of being abandoned."

It's a powerful moment when the pieces of the lens sentence puzzle suddenly snap together, capturing and explaining so many of your relationship's turbulent and troubling episodes. It's amazing to watch my clients' faces when their key words simply pop into their heads. This is how it all comes together. So, be prepared for an "aha!" moment.

Whatever feelings your lens sentence expresses, the sentence will be essential for the rest of the exercises in this book and a crucial device for retooling your relationship and achieving greater intimacy with your guy. I suggest that you write your lens sentence on a piece of paper using bright colors, make it into a fun banner to stick on the front cover of your notebook, or hide it in another private place away from your partner. This will serve as a gentle reminder for you to use it regularly as a way to focus and sharpen the significance of the thoughts, revelations, and changes you'll experience as you work through the exercises.

Many clients tell me that creating their lens sentence was one of the most powerful and even life-changing personal events they've ever experienced. They finally came to understand bad decisions, poor judgments, and self-defeating behavior, as well as feelings of rage, guilt, and sadness, by using this simple tool.

The beauty of the lens sentence is that it will be there for you long after you finish this book. In your life, the relationships you now have with your lover, family, and friends will change, evolve, and grow. Some of these relationships will move to the background, while others—some with people who have yet to appear—will take center stage. Ultimately, the choice is yours whether you continuously reenact the same set of life dramas and engage in the same unproductive behavior that you have since you were a kid. It's your chance to break free of the patterns that have been repeating in your family for generations.

Once you openly and consciously acknowledge your lens sentence and understand that it is the ultimate motivating emotion behind all and every conflict, issue, and dilemma you struggle with in all romantic relationships, you really don't have to do anything with it. You don't have to remind yourself constantly about it or repeat it to yourself when you walk into a club and begin to check out the scene or be mindful of it every time you have a conversation. When you understand and use your lens sentence, new perspectives and pathways in your relationship will open up to you, quite naturally and of their own volition. The retooling of your relationship has almost automatically begun. Your lens sentence is a gift that will reward you for a very long time. Why not celebrate and give yourself one of the badges, the presents you selected for yourself at the beginning of the book? You have now earned the understanding that you will carry with you—it's your badge of Insight.

PART TWO

Act Now to Retool Your Relationship

Romance and Intimacy: The Perfect Balance

If I were a genie and asked you to name one ingredient you'd like me to magically add to your relationship, what would you say? Most of my women clients wouldn't think twice. They would say that they'd like more romance. They would immediately conjure up the early days of their relationships as the ideal, a time when they felt as if their most intimate secrets, hopes, and dreams were freely, effortlessly, and openly shared. They would remember feeling that the connection to their men was so strong, so intuitive, that often words were not even necessary, because they could practically sense what the other was feeling. And the sex! It was so incredibly fulfilling, so all consuming. Yes, if somehow the intimacy of those first few weeks could be restored, then everything would be okay.

Intimacy Grows When We Feel Safe

If I really were a genie and could grant these women their wishes, I am sorry to say that they would be bitterly disappointed. Most women interpret the question "What is the one ingredient you want more of in your relationship?" in terms of something they experienced in the past, something they believe has been lost, which, if recovered, would make them feel satisfied and complete.

The only problem is that women (and men) often confuse intimacy—the kind that can sustain and nurture a relationship over time—with romance. This was often the case on *Tool Academy*. Most couples are not seeking the kind of intimacy that is an evolving, dynamic exchange of emotions and ideas; they want the kind they thought they experienced when their relationship was fresh: the romantic, "in love" feelings.

Real intimacy is much, much more than candlelight, holding hands while watching the sunset, and good sex (although these can be an excellent beginning). Real intimacy brings a kind of emotional security, the confidence that you can talk openly about yourself and reveal who you truly are, say whatever you want, and feel that you are really being heard by your partner. You both need to have a sense of humility and vulnerability. Intimacy is a two-way street, a kind of electrical circuit that runs between the two of you. A circuit that is completed only when the other person is as engaged and involved as you are. And that means he needs to be able to tell you when he feels frightened, inadequate, and powerless, instead of always pretending to be successful, in charge, and in control.

You've seen how the men on *Tool Academy* pump themselves up with their attitudes, smooth club speak, and stories of how hot they are to the opposite sex and how clever they are at getting girls' phone numbers. Yet it's pretty transparent that for all of their strutting, they are only covering up their feelings of weakness and inadequacy— feelings about themselves that they cannot bear to have others see. By episode three on the show, the Tools are as transparent as a window!

Being a woman, though, you have a head start. You intuitively have a more evolved sense of how to be intimate with a man. It's woven into your DNA. If you think about it, where would the human race be if women weren't born with the instinct of giving affection, care, attention, and protection to another member of the species?

Men are not so fortunate. Contrary to popular belief, men really do have deep feelings, experience vulnerability, and stumble under shouldering the burden of maintaining a facade of always being the tough guy. But they protect themselves from being swallowed up in a relationship by withdrawing, keeping emotionally aloof, and staying at a safe distance; they tend to fear intimacy.

And therein is the paradox that has plagued men and women since the beginning of time. In order for a woman to achieve the intimate, healthy relationship she wants, the man must be able to feel safe and reassured in expressing the one thing he is terrified of and totally inept at: being comfortable having and revealing his feelings.

Your Relationship Dance

Men associate intimacy with a loss of themselves, something they fear much more than women do. A woman, acting on her totally justifiable need for increased intimacy, naturally makes demands on her man, and nothing frightens a man more. For each step a woman tries to take toward her man, he takes two steps backward. It's a dance, really, one in which the woman is cast as the pursuer and the man plays the role of pursued.

In this session, you will learn how to coax your man out of his emotional cave and lure him into a safe and comfortable zone in which he feels more able to be himself. Soon, he'll not only accept your requests for greater intimacy, he'll begin to pursue you for them.

In order to take your relationship to this new state, however, you need to redefine the meaning of true intimacy.

Most people would describe intimacy using such words as "closeness," "togetherness," and "belonging." Yet even though this description is true, somewhat counterintuitively, intimacy also has boundaries. Let me explain. Because men have such an extreme fear of losing their manhood, their identity, their selves when entering into intimate relationships, they somehow misinterpret a woman's idea of intimacy as being totally consuming. In reality, nothing could be further from the truth.

No one—woman or man—wants to be so "intimate" as to lose herself or himself. How quickly would you start to feel suffocated if your man began to tag along with you 24/7, insisting on your eating all of your meals with him, accompanying you shopping, and wanting to inhabit your life? True, you want more intimacy in your relationship than you have now, certainly more than what's comfortable for him. Yet you don't want to be so close that your lives are fused and you can't tell where your feelings end and his begin— which is what your man is so frightened of.

The Perfect Distance between You and Your Man

With this in mind, I'd like you to consider a new definition of intimacy, one that I think you will find satisfying, as well as liberating. It is this: intimacy is the maximum degree of closeness in which a couple can coexist without each member losing his or her individuality. Your guy's chief worry is that he'll lose his individuality, while you, ironically, could probably use a booster shot of autonomy.

Healthy couples know how to actively maintain a unique distance between the two of them. They are able to achieve the optimal level of intimacy that they both find comfortable at any particular moment. True intimacy is not a static, stationary state. It shifts and moves continually, responding to the way both people feel. If you've had a bad day, your need to feel close to your man may be greater than on the evening when your best friend is in town just for the night. Intimacy is not two people at either end of a seesaw, holding each other in motionless balance. It's each person moving backward and forward on the seesaw, each responding, each initiating a response in order to find the right balance in a living, dynamic, ever-changing relationship.

The problem is that most couples *are* stuck. The man always withdraws, while the woman always pursues. As the man distances himself, the woman grows increasingly desirous and impatient for more intimacy until she often acts out her desires inappropriately, maybe by nagging, which drives her man farther back along the seesaw so that it tips up. As this behavior escalates, it can cause a woman to feel rejected. In couples, I often observe that the woman, after a period of being repeatedly pushed away, feels intensely—even irrationally—jealous. This scenario can unfold as a self-fulfilling prophecy because the man, unable to withdraw fast or far enough from his woman's incessant reproaches and demands, is actually propelled into an act of meaningless infidelity. The result is that the couple feels isolated, stifled, lonely, and unconnected.

To give you a better example of how this idea of Pursuer and Distancer might play itself out and how using your lens sentence can bring a fuzzy and volatile situation into focus, let me introduce you to Sara and Mark.

Sara and Mark initially came to me because they were having problems with sex. At first, they sat in stony silence and barely acknowledged each other's presence in the room. I encouraged them to speak freely and discuss their troubles openly. Sara kept looking at Mark out of the corner of her eye, slyly monitoring his face for a reaction. But Mark didn't register any emotion at first. It was clear that couples therapy was more Sara's idea than Mark's. He sat as if he were tolerating the situation. With a few days' growth on his cheeks, Mark came across as fashionably scruffy, his hair gelled up into tiny spikes, and it was clear he took pains to work out at the gym at every opportunity. I began by asking Mark what he wanted out of the therapy sessions, and when he didn't respond right away, Sara literally prodded him as if to say, "Go on, Mark, tell Trina everything." Mark started to talk but whenever he stopped mid-sentence, unable to find the right words or know exactly what to say, Sara always chimed in. I had to ask her not to put words into Mark's mouth.

I eventually pieced together that Mark had cheated on Sara the previous year, and although he thought they had worked it out and had moved forward, every so often Sara brought it up. It always ended with a huge fight and the decision to separate for a bit. Yet it wasn't too long before they would be texting, then talking again, and soon would be back together, following a night of drunken sex.

Sara grew very emotional as the session continued. Tears fell from her eyes that she didn't bother to wipe away, and she complained in a sorrowful voice how unloved and ignored she felt. Sara took Mark back, but as the months dragged on, he drifted further and further away emotionally, and eventually sex was dropped from the relationship altogether. That was the cue for Sara to have a few drinks too many and blurt out that she thought he must be having an affair again, because he obviously was not interested in her. She then relentlessly questioned him to learn the gory details of the last affair, rehashing all of the questions that Mark thought were ancient history.

In our sessions together, Sara complained of always having to chase Mark for any kind of romance, compliments, and togetherness. She felt that she had not really gotten over his affair but had somehow managed to bury it most of the time. Sometimes, however, the feelings simply boiled up, and, not being able to contain them any longer, Sara and Mark had the inevitable fight that both of them had known was coming.

Mark's story was that he felt crowded by Sara's constant demands for attention. At the same time, he was worried that he was not enough for her. Mark felt very guilty about having cheated, but it did provide him with a sense of comfort and a much-needed break from Sara's incessant demands.

Instead of being able to modify their relationship, they agreed it would be easier to split up and give it a break for a while. It was always Sara who managed to get them talking again, because she could not imagine life without him. But no sooner did they get back together than the same pattern would assert itself, with Sara feeling insecure and making demands and Mark feeling hassled and therefore withdrawing.

Both Sara and Mark struggled with regulating a level of intimacy that permitted them to operate from a comfortable zone of closeness. Mark was secretly worried that he was a failure. His dad had been fired from his job at forty and never found real employment again, leaving his mother resentful and angry. Mark was very worried about his job security and interpreted Sara's pressure for closeness as a threat. The men in Mark's family all had trouble holding down jobs for any meaningful length of time, and from his perspective, Mark believed that if Sara got close to him, she would also see him as a failure and leave him forever. Part of the experience of being close to another person is being able to deal with the risk of "being found out," "discovered," and "exposed." When Mark wandered off to have his affair, it was with a woman who was much older than him, with whom he felt reassured and safe.

Mark's lens sentence was "I always disappoint." It came as no surprise to me, really, that it was so similar to Sara's, which was "I am never good enough." Sara was the youngest child of five children growing up in a household of busy, high-achieving parents who had very little time for her. She did badly at school, and it always seemed that her brothers and sisters stole the special times with her parents, what little there ever was of it. Sara's lens sentence came true when Mark had his affair, and now she was trying to repair the damage to her relationship by desperately trying to be "good enough."

The String Thing

Imagine Mark and Sara's relationship as a length of string between them. Sara was the one to pull on it to bring Mark closer, and Mark, feeling the string getting too short, was the one to drop it and run.

The phenomenon of the Pursuer/Distancer couple has many variations. Although it is more common that the woman does the pursuing, the roles can be reversed. The dynamics between the two, however, are always the same. One member chases the other, while the other gets as far away as possible. In both cases, each person is acting out his or her own lens sentence. And as is so often the case, both members of the couple have the same lens sentence! Take, for example, Tanya and Peter.

Everything about the way Tanya dressed and composed herself told me that she was a professional woman who liked to keep busy. I could see that she applied her makeup very carefully, and she wore her fine blond hair combed into a tight ponytail. She made a point of turning off her two cell phones moments after the session officially began. Her demeanor—the way she crossed her legs and looked me straight in the eye—signaled that here was a woman who meant business. From the get-go, she introduced herself by saying she was a paralegal in a high-powered law firm. And although the position demanded long hours and often required her to work on weekends, she was quite satisfied with the job because she considered it a stepping-stone to a higher-paying position in the firm and a satisfying career. When Tanya wasn't in the office, she was at her mother's house, helping her do chores and just chatting. Her boyfriend, Peter, didn't share or understand Tanya's ambition or passion for work. He put up with Tanya's preoccupations at first but soon began to feel neglected, unappreciated, and resentful. Having an excess of free time, Peter began to hang out at bars and soon found himself deep in an affair.

It wasn't long before Tanya found out because Peter made it very obvious by staying out late and coming home with lame excuses.

Tanya confronted Peter, and when he admitted the affair, Tanya quickly forgave him, begged him to stay, and became very attentive. She dropped the extra hours at work and saw less of her mother. Yet her obliging behavior lasted only a couple of months before she felt smothered and constrained in the relationship. She asked for and was granted a transfer to another branch of her office, 250 miles away. She found temporary lodgings and came home on the weekends. Had Peter been given the opportunity to move, he probably would have turned it down, by saying that there were no good job opportunities for him in the new area. But Tanya never gave him the option. She announced her transfer and the new living arrangements, and that was that.

Tanya and Peter's story comes into focus when you learn a little more about their backgrounds. Peter's father had abandoned his family, leaving Peter to be raised by a single mother until he became too much for her and was adopted by an older, childless couple. Tanya was the longed-for child, also of older parents, who smothered her with love and attention to the point that she felt quite overwhelmed by them.

When it came time for them to write their lens sentences, they were surprised to discover that they had written the same sentence: "I am afraid of being on my own." Peter was frightened of being abandoned by Tanya, as he had been by his birth mother. And Tanya was frightened of being alone, because her parents had never left her alone in her life. She always had an exit strategy, a plan to get away, to derail intimate moments because they reminded her of her suffocating parents. But when she did get away, she felt unloved and frightened.

If you imagine this couple's relationship as a string, with each partner at either end, they would constantly be going back and forth, unable to find a suitable balance. Peter would grab hold of the string and try to pull Tanya closer. Each time he did, she would let out more string so that he would get farther and farther away. As they sorted out the connections to their past with me in therapy, they were able to see that they were reacting as if they were still the children in their families. They agreed to try to tolerate the demands of being more intimate in their present lives now that they both understood and could trust each other not to leave.

I hope that the stories of Sara and Mark and Tanya and Peter have helped you visualize a new way to think about the subject of intimacy in your relationship. If you regard intimacy as a string connecting you to your partner, you will quickly realize how the turbulence in your relationship can be considered a kind of dance. Every time you pull on the string to bring your man closer, he responds by letting out a length of string from his side. Or the same thing can happen, but the other way around. Every time your guy pulls on his side of the string to bring you closer, you let out a section of string to keep him at what you consider to be a safe distance.

And so it goes. For every one step you take toward him, he takes two steps backward. For every two steps he takes toward you, you take two steps forward, making him step away again. It's a perpetual dance that leads to frustration, disappointment, anger, and resentment. Some couples never find a fluid harmony—the give and take—that brings the relationship into balance and results in true, sustainable intimacy. Yet if you realize that all couples have a perfect distance in their relationship that at any given moment can be actively maintained, then you can achieve the level of intimacy you truly desire by being in control of the string.

EXERCISE

String Theory

To help you take control of your intimacy string, I've developed a useful exercise over the years that will let you manage the fluid balance of closeness that you seek.

With your relationship in mind, find a piece of string, a thread, or a chain that most closely represents the kind of attachment you have with your man. Really think about how the two of you relate on a day-to-day basis, and then go on a scavenger hunt around the house for the kind of string that best represents your relationship. Is it a bit of elastic band because you are always being stretched and bouncing back? It is a cotton thread from a piece of clothing, because a good, sharp tug can snap it in two? Is it picture-hanging wire that is able to hold up heavy objects? A piece of twine made out of individual, easily breakable strands that when woven together are incredibly strong? What about a jewelry chain, its strength composed of individual links? Is it made of silk, gold, leather, or lace? When you decide on your string, save it with your lens sentence at the front of your notebook, and jot down a few phrases of dialogue between you and your partner that capture the style of your "string" attachment.

The Attachment Dance

Now that you've thought about your particular style of attachment, I'd like you to spend some time during this session experimenting with it. This will require you to notice how you and your partner are pulling and lengthening your relationship string. For example, at breakfast, maybe you suggest going out to a movie together after work, but when he comes home from the office, he chooses that particular evening to clean out the garage. Or when you mention the possibility of taking a long drive over the upcoming three-day holiday weekend, he announces a few days later that he's made plans for a camping trip with his buddies. Or maybe instead of celebrating your birthday by taking you out for a romantic dinner at your favorite restaurant, he tells you he's invited his family over for dinner.

I've found that occasionally some women find it difficult to recognize conduct that I would characterize as pursuing behavior. They refuse to think of their actions as an attempt to chase their men; after all, they are only attempting to gain a greater measure of closeness and make the relationship better. Thinking of themselves as pursuers is too negative a label. Yet it is important to understand your behavior, without judging yourself harshly or hanging negative connotations on yourself. Remember that all relationships experience the back and forth of the Pursuer/Distancer dance. Examples of it can occur multiple times and with varying degrees of intensity within a single conversation. The Pursuer/Distancer dance is built into the very nature of a relationship, or, to put it another way, it exists within the relationship and as an integral part of it. The key isn't to stop the dance entirely, because not only is it impossible to do so, it would also harm the existing relationship further. The point is to gain control of the dance and the "intimacy string length" so that within the fluid gathering-up-and-letting-go of your relationship string, you can coax your boyfriend to be more intimate, pull on the string, shorten the string a little, and so fulfill your needs.

One of the more common pursuing behaviors you've probably tried is attempting to talk to your guy about your need to have greater intimacy in the relationship. In my experience, talking about wanting a closer relationship usually ends up going nowhere. The man feels pressured and withdraws even further, and the woman feels rebuffed, angry, and frustrated. This is sometimes followed by feelings of guilt and self-recrimination on both sides. So, after a few negative experiences of trying to get him to talk about the relationship, many women go into self-protection mode and suppress the need to talk about it. You may have learned the hard way that insisting on a conversation about intimacy usually leads to a fight and leaves you feeling horrible and even ashamed. This self-censoring works for a while until the situation simply gets the better of you, and all of a sudden, there you go again, blurting out the one thing you promised yourself you'd never do, demanding an answer to the question "Do you really love me?"

Your fear of being labeled a nagger, a whiner, or a weak and clutching woman has bottled up the hurt inside you. Uncontainable, it erupts in the form of a highly threatening and aggressive question that sends him running. He may respond by saying rather flatly,

"Yes, I do love you." But you know him well enough to see that he is feeling guilty, besieged, and trapped, and nothing he says can lessen your feelings of distance.

Here is one more example of a behavior that may not be recognizable as pursuing at first glance. Many of the women I meet in my practice have sacrificed areas of their personal lives in the belief that making themselves more available will convert into more meaningful intimate moments with their partners. It is a mistake women often make. They stop taking night classes to advance their careers, give up hobbies they enjoy, and excuse themselves from a girls' night out with friends, all in the hope of having more quality time with their partners. But this kind of compromise cleverly conceals a form of Pursuer behavior. Many women sacrifice activities they enjoy as a form of emotional collateral, something they do with the expectation that their men will reciprocate and devote more of themselves to the relationship.

Unfortunately, it rarely turns out that way. When you have more available time to pull on his string, he finds new ways to distance himself. And so it goes on. It's a common mistake to think that by compromising yourself, you can engender intimacy. Often the gesture goes unrecognized, which only adds to the cycle of pursuit and withdrawal.

When I hear the lengths that some of my clients go to in trying to meet the needs of their men or, more accurately, what they perceive to be the needs of their men, I tell them that they've already compromised enough. Many express relief because they assumed that I was going to prescribe that they compromise more. Remember that we are defining true intimacy as the degree in which each member of the couple is able to be close but also preserve his or her individual identity at the same time. You need to engage in activities you enjoy outside the relationship. It follows quite naturally that by pursuing activities that define, develop, and strengthen your selfhood, this will also enable you to find the space to enjoy the intimacy you require within your relationship.

Observe Your Dance

Now that you are sensitized to the many and various ways you and your partner dance around your need for (and his fear of) intimacy, it's time to experiment a little. I want you to notice how you react when you begin to pull on your relationship string, and he starts to withdraw. Do you stamp your feet and act angry? Do you argue and try to reason with him? Do you tell him how disappointed you feel? Remember, the purpose of this exercise is to notice how your string is actually working within the relationship. So, at this stage, try to take the stance of an observer and watch how you act and feel when he lets out lengths of his relationship string. Write down your observations in your notebook.

EXERCISE

Control Your Dance

In this exercise I want you to do the following: when you feel him withdrawing, instead of behaving in your customary manner, try a different response. Instead of taking another step toward him, try taking a step backward and wait. The trick is to distance yourself just at the moment you would normally pursue. It will take a bit of discipline on your part. It will be at a time when your lens sentence is activated and your vulnerability rises to the surface. So, the next time he begins to distance himself, you'll recognize what is happening and, instead of stepping nearer, try to step away and wait. If he distances again, step away again and wait. If he comes toward you, do not go toward him, but step away again.

For example, instead of reminding him that he promised to hang out with you when he is heading to the gym, act indifferent and detached. Or, instead of insisting that he tell you what time he'll be back from his bar hopping with his buddies, try a simple, "Okay, 'bye! Have fun!" It's going to feel a bit weird at first, because you are so used to reacting in a routine way. But give it a try. If he distances himself again, step away again. And wait. If he comes toward you, no matter how you feel, step back. And wait.

Let Out the String!

When doing this exercise, you may feel as if you are getting nowhere fast and that he can outdistance you. You may feel like you are not moving any closer to him, while his string is getting longer and longer. Yet there will be a point where he will stop retreating and will take a step toward you. People who are Distancers also have to be Pursuers or the relationship wouldn't exist in the first place. Remember that our definition of intimacy is the degree of closeness in which a couple can coexist without each member losing his or her individuality. It becomes safe for the Distancer to keep pulling away because he knows that his Pursuer partner will come after him and maintain the relationship. He will have to come closer eventually to maintain your attachment, so sit tight. Act blasé and indifferent. Make him sweat a little. Worry him enough so that he feels the distance growing and then watch him start pulling on his string to bring you closer.

When he comes in late, act normally without anger. If he spends all weekend watching sports on television and in the evening goes upstairs to play games on the computer, don't confront him. You'll feel completely ignored, left out, and steaming mad. He is letting out your string big-time! But this time, you are aware of it. So, just this week, you are going to take yourself happily off to bed and curl up with a good book, or dress up and go out with your best girl-friend. I guarantee that he will make a very unusual move toward you before much time passes. He will come out of his cave and ask what you are up to or whether you want to go out to dinner. Or he may offer to drive you to the mall. Watch for it. He will exhibit a behavior that he knows you will appreciate, one that he knows you will recognize as bringing him closer to you.

You may have to wait quite a while, and it may test your patience. When he begins to pursue you, however, don't give in right away. Keep your distance until you are satisfied that he is actively pursuing you. When he does, don't jump all over him, or you will undo all of your good work. Simply be intimate and close, enjoy the connection, and then disconnect again. Maybe you can excuse yourself and go into the kitchen to make a cup of coffee or grab the car keys and run down to the grocery store before it closes. You are showing him that you are independent and okay on your own by slipping off to Skype your traveling friend for several hours or saying that you really must visit your mom. You are still in the dance, but the difference is that you are now leading it.

Lure Him out of His Cave

We all are more able to love and care for another when we feel understood and safe. I know this is what you want him to do for you, but how you've been going about it hasn't worked, has it? By now, I suspect that your man is in his cave, quite withdrawn and uncommunicative. Even when you are sharing the sofa, it's as if the two of you are miles apart. There is a hollow, empty feeling that you can't shake. Besides, you are emotionally on edge all of the time because you never know when the tiniest, most innocent comment is going to trigger an argument.

This exercise will change all of that. You are going to create a safe, neutral environment in which greater intimacy is possible, where your man can acknowledge your needs, listen to your concerns, and be in a position to respond favorably. It is designed to coax him out of his protective shell and lure him into a secure and comfortable environment, so that he'll be more willing and available to return the intimacy and feelings of closeness that you are giving him.

The Three Gifts

For this exercise, you will give your man three "gifts," and further-more, he won't know they are gifts! Of course, *you* will know they are gifts, and I want you to carefully observe your partner's behav-ior in the subsequent hours or days after they are received. He'll notice that you are doing things differently. He'll think something's up. He'll suspect that things in the relationship are changing. He'll wonder to himself, Why is she acting this way? Is something wrong with us?

Gift giving isn't as easy as it sounds. You may also say that you have already given him enough gifts, but I'm guessing that they have not been without your expecting something in return, and the gifts were certainly not given by the new you who is reading this book. I often hear couples talk about all of the things they do for each other, but none of it is what their partners actually want. Once a guy in a couple I was helping began to pat himself on the back for picking up his girlfriend from work each day, only to have her chime in that she hated these rides because she felt as if he was checking up on her, controlling her. So be sure that the three gifts you pick are things that you know he wants. These gifts are for him, not for you. Be certain they are things you know he likes and will appreciate, not what you want him to have or what will make you feel good to give. Again, as you learned in session 1, it's all about speaking the same language. If you don't know the kinds of gifts he wants, then carefully check in with him. Listen closely to his conversation, to what he appreciates and compliments about others. If you have been paying attention and actively listening to him, you'll probably think of your three gift ideas very quickly. Remember, you are undercover. Be stealthy. You wouldn't want him to suspect anything at this point in the game!

Also bear in mind that the kinds of gifts I am talking about are not necessarily the store-bought variety. The right gifts are not the big, expensive kind. And they are not necessarily the sexual kind. They might not even be consciously noticed. Think of your three gifts as actions or activities.

Some good gift ideas include the following:

1. Buy him a bar of chocolate.
2. Send him a little love note with his packed lunch.
3. Call him at work just to say hi.
4. Kiss him before you leave in the morning.
5. Plan for the two of you to go away for a weekend as a surprise.
6. Say a big thank-you for something he has done.
7. Massage his feet.
8. Boast to a friend in front of him about something wonderful he has done.
9. Watch his favorite TV show with him.
10. Make love with him.
11. Make him his favorite meal.
12. Give him a CD of his favorite music.
13. Run a bath for him.
14. Say "I love you" to him several times during the day.
15. Really listen while he tells you about his bad day.
16. Send him sexy text messages.
17. Take his dog for a walk.
18. Give him that item of clothing he said he was saving up for.
19. Participate in his favorite outdoor activity.
20. Send him an e-mail at work saying he is gorgeous.
21. Give him a back rub.

22. Let him laze around in bed on a Saturday morning.

23. Run your fingers through his hair.

24. Give him the book he's been wanting.

25. Tell him you want him to go on that weekend with his buddies after all.

26. Put gas in his car.

27. Give him a framed photograph of his dog.

Bear in mind that his lens sentence is probably very similar to yours, so when you think up your three gifts, apply your lens sentence. Think about whether his reaction to the gift you are considering giving him would stop him from feeling that his lens sentence is always being activated. If your lens sentence is "I feel insecure about myself," then remember that his will be similar. Your gift will help make him feel better about himself, more safe and secure; it will put him in a better frame of mind to give you in return the intimacy you deserve.

Be SMART

This tip will help ensure that the gifts you choose will successfully achieve your desired objective of creating a neutral environment in which he can initiate the kind of intimate behavior you seek.

For each gift idea you consider, put it to the SMART test.

Specific: Be sure the gift is something concrete, tangible, and physical. Something he can detect with his senses. Think through exactly what the gift is before you present him with it. Don't try to improvise or make it up along the way.

Measurable: Your gift should be an object or an activity that has a discrete quantity assigned to it. For example, if you choose number 26, "Put gas in his car," plan in advance when you are going to do it. Before work? After the weekend?

Achievable: Don't select a gift that you are not capable of giving. If there is an activity you know he would enjoy but, for one reason or another, you are incapable of or uncomfortable going through with it, then pass it over. There are plenty of gifts your guy will enjoy. Don't set yourself up for failure by selecting a gift that is beyond your pocketbook or your emotional limits.

Realistic: Many gifts would be wonderful to give but are simply unrealistic because they are too elaborate, too expensive, too lavish, or too excessive. These types of gifts easily backfire, not only because they are a dead giveaway that you are trying too hard and they will arouse suspicion in your man, but also because the inappropriateness of the gift will be obvious and will ultimately embarrass both you and your partner. Realistic gifts make the best gifts.

Time limited: Your gifts need to have limits. If they are activities, like calling him at work to say hi, then you must consider the appropriate time to call and how often to call, lest your gift become a nuisance. Let your call be a rare and pleasant surprise, not something that interrupts him in a meeting or makes him think you're checking up on him. You can apply this principle to other types of gifts, too. Nothing remains pleasurable if it goes on indefinitely. Besides, the success of this exercise depends on it having a stopping point or a limit. That way, you are placed in a position of control, and you will have him just where you want him, begging for more.

Watch, Look, Listen

Remember what I said about the importance of being an observer in your own relationship? Again, it is crucial that you notice where and when you presented your gifts, how you gave them, and, most important, how they were received. You need to maintain your observer status for the rest of the session, keeping a vigilant eye on the little ways his behavior is changing. He may act puzzled, amusedly suspicious, pleasantly aroused, or even silly.

Write down in your notebook all of these details to describe how your boyfriend is acting. Don't let on about what you are doing. It is vital that you make no mention of the gifts in any way that could be construed as their being a favor, as collateral for future payback, or as if you expect anything in return. They are gifts, given freely and without obligation.

What you've accomplished is establishing more balance in your dance, by helping him feel secure enough to pull you closer. You have achieved this important step by staying in control and without his knowledge.

By creating a secure environment for him, you can expect his defenses to drop and for him to begin to take little tugs on your string, bringing you closer. It will happen, believe me! He may surprise you in the middle of the day with a spontaneous phone call. He may suggest accompanying you on a shopping errand. He may even initiate a session of lovemaking.

Intimacy Checkup

By the end of this session, you should begin to see small changes in your relationship and in your man. The changes may be difficult to notice at first, but once you've picked up on them, they will be impossible to ignore. Now is a good time to check back with yourself and gauge the progress you've made.

- Go back and retrieve the piece of string you placed in the front of your notebook. Has the idea of your string changed at all? Would you select the same string now if you had a chance to choose again?

- Can you control the distance between yourself and your man? Are you in control of your string and can you let it out whenever you choose?

- What have you learned about your dancing style? How does it influence the way you interact with your man?

- Do you feel more in control? More independent? Have you been thinking about your own needs outside of the relationship?

- Has your lovemaking changed? Can you use the string theory to control your behavior, while having sex in such a way that he acts more intimately or pursues you more aggressively in the ways you want?

You've given your guy plenty of wonderful gifts in this session; now it's time for you to give yourself one. Select one of the special pleasures you previously itemized, and think of it as your Intimacy badge.

You've come a long way, but his distancing habits won't disappear overnight. Disagreements will pop up, no matter how close a couple is. Contrary to common belief, arguments can provide a woman with an opportunity to take charge and transform a confrontation into a close and caring encounter. And that's what's next.

Arguing Effectively with Your Tool

I f you're not in a struggle, you're not in a relationship! Relationships are supposed to be difficult; otherwise, it would be impossible for us to learn, change, and grow as people. But what if your guy doesn't seem to be doing a lot of growing? He may be so absorbed, satisfying his own self-centered needs, appetites, and fun, that you sometimes feel as if you're the mother and he's just a grown-up little boy. Take, for example, what happens when he doesn't get his way. He sulks, mopes, or flies into a tantrum, making you wish you could pack him off to his mother's so that you could enjoy some grown-up fun with your girlfriends.

You're the mature one, handling the ups and downs of everyday existence, recognizing and meeting the challenges life throws at you on a daily basis, keeping your hands tightly on the wheel so that the relationship doesn't end up in a ditch.

Most of the time you cope with his bad behavior toward you. You find the patience to put up with his insensitive little remarks about the way you look, the household chores he says he'll do but never gets around to, or the way he always seems to put his own friends first. But sometimes, he can be such a conceited, arrogant Tool that you feel as if you have no other option but to lose it, so that he will stop whatever he's doing and pay attention to what you tell him.

Yet instead of listening, he puts on an expression that says, "Hey, what's your problem?" And that really does it. That's all the push you need to pass through being merely irritated, skip over being offended, and arrive at full-fledged anger.

Then he starts in. Suddenly, he's dredging up arguments about stuff you thought was long dead and buried. He's blaming you, all over again, for not taking his side in an argument at a party. He's condemning you for criticizing him in front of your parents last Christmas. And can you really fault him for it? From his perspective, your censure is coming out of the blue. After all, he's only human—and a man at that. He'll do what any man would do under similar circumstances: go on the offensive.

At this point, the energy can go one of two ways. Wishing to restore some semblance of normalcy, some women withdraw entirely and protect themselves behind the shield of their own psyche, unable to defuse their partners' rage. Other women go on the attack, giving as good as they get, willing to take the altercation to the wall and let the pieces of the wreckage fall where they may.

Unfortunately, I've seen these scenarios play out all too many times, and they always end by exacerbating the hurt feelings that the argument was intended to resolve. Whether a woman responds by retreating into herself or with aggressive behavior, she has unwittingly reinforced the same familiar cycle of feeling isolated, unappreciated, and misunderstood, which causes her to suppress even more anger that threatens to come to the surface the next time he provokes her.

Anger can be a great catalyst for change, if you know how to use it. The problem for most women is that they don't possess the tools to use their anger to argue effectively, take control of the situation, and get what they want. Often, the cause of the argument is entirely legitimate, but the way women go about expressing themselves leads them down a dangerous path toward more hurt and bitterness. If you knew how to safely acknowledge and effectively communicate pain, you'd never need to get angry. (Of course, this applies to him, too.)

How to Fight

As with all of the sessions in the book, with the exception of session 2, you should read through each one thoroughly before actually attempting to do any of the exercises. Each exercise is a small step leading to a big one. To be successful, you need to understand where you are headed before you set out on the journey.

In this session, you'll learn the techniques to express your anger without totally giving in to it, enabling you to stay in control of your man and any argument. You will learn how to hold the power in the relationship, gradually create a calm and rational environment, and conduct negotiations in a language he understands to get what you want and deserve.

And how, exactly, will you accomplish this miraculous feat?

You are going to spend the next few days arguing, really going at it. These disagreements may be about things you've argued about before, or they may be a rehash of issues that keep coming back in the relationship. Make no mistake, you will really be arguing, not just playing at it. Tempers will flare on both sides. I guarantee that there will be a lot of nastiness flung about, except that this time you're going to stage these quarrels in such a way that you'll be in control, teaching him how to listen, understand, and change his behavior toward you. And the beauty of it is that he won't even realize he's being guided into giving you what you want.

I've noticed from my private practice and from *Tool Academy* that whenever a woman listens to herself describe her grown man throwing fits, stomping around the living room, or moping in a corner, she is able to realize that her guy is acting like a small child when he doesn't get what he wants. She suddenly understands that the adult man she's living with utterly lacks the maturity to understand, control, or express what's really bothering him. He's too absorbed in his own emotions, unable to even recognize the feelings that run riot inside him, much less empathize with hers.

This concept is empowering in itself, but it still leaves you dealing with an angry man-child, instead of the knight in shining armor you thought you were getting. Well, put on your own armor, get up on your white horse, and prepare to lead the charge, because it's now up to you to bring him to heel, get him to act like an adult, and be prepared to discuss, listen, understand, and, most important, fulfill your needs for intimacy.

Feel the Power of Your Communication

I'd like to give you a quickie exercise to allow you to flex your muscles and feel the power you already possess to control a conversation with your man. It will give you just the merest inkling of the secret weapon you have, with your body language alone.

Here's how it goes. The next time you are at the dinner table or sitting on the sofa together, keep an ear open for when he goes off on a monologue about his day. Perhaps he'll start to talk about his escapades with his pals at the club last night or will ramble on in minute detail about how he scored the winning basket during a pick-up game with his friends. Instead of acting like you usually do, muttering the occasional "uh-huh" and nodding your head when he pauses to see whether you are listening, this time simply break eye contact without saying a word. Let your gaze wander about the room, perhaps settling on a picture over his shoulder on the opposite wall or maybe on the tree outside the window. Let your inner actress take over. Fidget. Sigh. Cough. Tap your fingers and look bored. Check e-mails or text messages on your cell phone.

The result will be that he'll continue to talk for a moment or two, then—wait for it—he will suddenly stop speaking. He will lose his concentration; his monologue will grind to a halt.

He'll shift conversational gears entirely and ask you what's wrong, why aren't you paying attention, are you feeling all right? He'll feel frustrated, naturally, and a little irritation will probably creep into his voice. He will wonder what you are doing, but don't let on! The point is, he won't be able to continue talking, and you've successfully demonstrated to yourself the power you already have to control communication with your guy. You interrupted his pattern and threw him off guard. Suddenly, he's no longer in control. You've just changed the game, and change is the most crucial element of evolution in a relationship.

I urge you to try this. It's not enough for you to believe it works merely because I say so. Have a go at it. Prove it to yourself. But remember, this is only an exercise to reinforce your belief in your powers to change your relationship single-handedly. It's not intended to bring about a change in the relationship and is not something that I recommend you repeat. It is simply an appetizer for the main course that will come later in this session.

The ABCs of Your XYZ

As I mentioned earlier, most women in dysfunctional relationships use anger as a way to get their men's attention, engage with the men, and get themselves heard. It rarely works. It is easy to see how a mild disagreement can quickly escalate into an F5 tornado. All the woman has to work with is a vocabulary of anger to express what's troubling her and to communicate how she wants him to make it better. In this next warm-up exercise, I'll help you acquire verbal techniques to effectively express what he's done to upset you, tell him in a way that he can understand, and make it possible for him to change his behavior so that it doesn't happen again.

• •

Open Your Notebook

I'm going to provide three scenarios involving couples, in which the man unintentionally angers his partner. In the first two scenarios I have given you examples of how the woman might have responded to the man by phrasing her sentences in this way: "When you did X, it made me feel Y; please, would you do Z instead?" After reading the third scenario, put yourself in the place of the woman and fill in the X, Y, and Z in the sentence as you think she would have answered.

Scenario 1, The Restaurant Snub: Last night, Megan and Josh went out for dinner. Shortly after being seated, quite by chance, Josh spotted a college buddy at the bar and invited him over. They quickly began to reminisce about their old girlfriends, laughing and telling stories. Although they were clearly having a good time, Josh did not bring Megan into the conversation, practically kept his back to her the entire evening, and left her with no one to talk to.

As soon as they returned home, she confronted him: "Next time you want a date, why don't you just call up one of your old girlfriends and see if she's not busy?" Or maybe she said, "Don't ever, ever do that again. Don't invite me out to dinner and just ignore me." Or, "Why did you do that to me? I felt so insulted that you wouldn't even talk to me. Are you ashamed of me, is that it?"

By venting her hurt feelings in anger, framing them in sarcastic accusations or as an injured victim, Megan has doomed any possible satisfactory resolution of her complaint. The atmosphere is poisoned. The environment is already supercharged with tension, and there is no chance of their engaging in a rational discussion that she can control to get her needs met.

Now, referring to the XYZ sentence above, one approach might have been for Megan to say, "When you didn't include me in the conversation (X), it made me feel pushed to the side and put down (Y); next time, would you include me in the discussion?" (Z) This way, she is letting Josh know that she found his behavior unacceptable, and she says it in a way that is emotionally neutral, without accusation, and acceptable to him. It's important to emphasize that she is also telling him how to correct the situation should it ever arise again. Remember, Megan is not asking for an apology or a reason for his behavior. Her focus is on changing how Josh acts from this moment onward, not on getting him to say, "I'm sorry," for something that has already happened and that he probably wouldn't acknowledge was wrong. By making it crystal clear how she experienced his behavior and how it made her feel, she is also instructing him how she wants him to act the next time.

Scenario 2, Breaking a Promise: Kaitlyn and Eric live together and are engaged to be married. For the third month in a row, Eric has neglected to pay the gas bill. While tidying up, Kaitlyn discovered a notice of service termination on his nightstand. She and Eric have a long-standing mutual agreement that he would pay the monthly gas bill, while she would be responsible for the electric bill, which she has paid each month without fail. Kaitlyn is angry that Eric has broken his promise and not held up his end of the deal. She feels that she is quite alone, fulfilling all of the responsibilities of running the household.

If Kaitlyn was using the XYZ technique, she might say, "When you don't pay the gas bill, I feel upset, so please either pay the bill on time, or tell me if you can't afford it that month." Or she might say, "When you did not pay the gas bill, it made me feel really disappointed. Please, pay it regularly, or let me know if there's a problem." Or, if the woman was Anna from session 3, she might say, "I know this sounds a bit dramatic, but when you don't pay the gas bill on time, I feel abandoned, as if you don't care about our lives, our home, and me. If you can pay the bill on time next month, I will feel that you really do care about our lives together and are committed to us."

Scenario 3, Taking Advantage of You: Rachel works long hours at her job, and tonight she's come home after an exhausting day. Not only was her boss in a bad mood, her coworkers shunted off their work on her, and she missed lunch. As she comes through the kitchen door, she sees a stack of dirty dishes in the sink. She knows that when she left this morning, she cleaned up the breakfast dishes and that her boyfriend, Jonathan, has been home all day. This has happened before, and she hasn't said anything about it, but now Jonathan's chronic inability to pick up after himself has gotten to her, big-time.

Now it's your turn. Complete the XYZ sentence in your notebook, filling in what you might say if the situation were to happen to you: "When you did X, it made me feel Y; would you please do Z instead?"

• •

An important benefit of the XYZ sentence is that it removes you to a comfortable distance from which to safely and clearly express your feelings and negotiate a resolution of the conflict. The XYZ sentence enables you to inhabit the role of an observer, rather than a sorely wronged and much-maligned participant. By avoiding the role of victim—and him the part of perpetrator—you have taken the first step on the road to taking charge. Healthy couples always have a relationship about their relationship. The next time he exhibits a behavior that you want to change, remember to be a good journalist by reporting the vulnerable feelings you are experiencing. Don't begin your requests with, "You always . . ." or "You never . . ." Finish your request by clearly and concisely insisting on what sort of behavior change you want to see from him and how it would make you feel.

When you try this exercise for yourself, expect your partner to argue or object to what he considers factual descriptions of the incident. If that happens, I want you to remember that no one has the right to question your own experience; it is something no one can devalue or take away from you. He may not think you've got the right "take" on things or that you're not seeing the situation from his perspective. All of that is pretty much beside the point, though. Insist on the truth of your own feelings. After all, he can't dispute how you feel. What is important is that he acknowledges your perspective, which he will if it is delivered in a neutral, unthreatening way, using your XYZ sentence. In short order, without his realizing it, you will make your man hear you in a new and different way.

Let Your Tempers Flare

Now that you have experienced the power you already possess to shape the course of a conversation with your partner and you have the verbal technique to create a neutral, rational environment in which to have your needs heard and met, you are ready for the main exercise of the session.

As you might have guessed, I would like you to have an argument every day for about a week (you probably are already, if you are reading this book). You might be arguing most of the time or perhaps only in brief spurts. Maybe when you fight, you know how to back off, and the arguments are light and short. Or you are selective and pick the arguments carefully, knowing exactly where and when to dig in your heels. But this session is about getting control of the argument, modulating its intensity, and directing its outcome, without his knowledge or agreement.

So now is the time to really go for it and give it your best shot. Wait and watch for something he does that really pisses you off and call him on it. Is he spending another night down in the basement replacing the brakes on his beloved motorcycle, instead of paying attention to you up in the bedroom? Did he invite his brother over to the house again for Saturday night dinner, which will end up as it always does, with you playing hostess to the two of them as they're parked on the sofa in front of the TV?

Don't hold back. Really let him have it with both barrels. Let the intensity of the argument escalate. Allow the long-repressed resentments to rise to the surface. Remember, it is possible to have a "good" argument. It can be one of the most intimate moments a couple will share, when each person is totally and fiercely engaged and committed to the other. But it can also be one of the most dangerous.

The key is to keep the argument productive by staying in control. The way to stay in control is to hold back a little from the action so that you don't lose yourself in the heat of the disagreement to the point where all perspective is gone. In this exercise, I will show you how to keep a piece of yourself in reserve so that you can accurately track what's being said between the two of you and monitor the emotional temperature of the verbal exchange. Remember: it is important to keep yourself detached from the battle, so that you'll be able to stay in command.

Whenever you sense that the temperature of the argument has risen to a dangerous level and emotions are about to boil over, disconnect from the situation. And I mean literally. Announce to your partner that you feel that the situation is about to get out of hand, that you are going to step out for a moment, but you promise to return. Simply declare a time-out. This is critical. You must tell him that although you are leaving, you'll be back shortly—and you must honor this promise.

Physically remove yourself by going into another room, taking a walk around the block, or sitting on the porch. When you feel your sense of stability and perspective return, seek out your partner and—yes—pick up where you left off, checking first that he has calmed down, too.

Most people actually forget to come back and finish the argument, fearful of the emotions and the harsh words that have been flying everywhere. They mistakenly believe that it is better to call a truce and are pleased with themselves to have the relationship once again assume a semblance of normalcy, however temporary it may be. But I'm asking you to take a risk, live on the edge, get in there, and stick with it. You are now very close to achieving the fulfillment of your emotional requirements in the relationship. No compromise. No negotiation. No surrender.

Call as many time-outs as are necessary, then resume talking. And while you are catching your emotional breath (and he, his), review what just happened between the two of you. I don't mean rehashing in your mind the offensive behavior that sparked the argument or giving yourself a pep talk that you are in the right and he is in the wrong. I'd like you to pinpoint the exact words that almost pushed the argument over the edge and caused the time-out. What was it that he said, then you said, then he said, then you said? If you'd like to, write this in your notebook. When you come back into the room, begin the conversation with what brought the argument to its melting point. But this time, all of the emotion will be drained from the words, and you can continue to work toward a resolution. You can now use the XYZ technique to express your annoyance, concerns, and desire for change. In this way, the renewed conversation has begun on the right foot, with your taking control.

What will happen, I guarantee it, is that soon the two of you will be talking rationally. He'll be able to hear your objections, and you'll be able to convey how you feel and tell him how you want him to behave, because you have used your XYZ sentence.

You have maintained control of your arguments and have steered them to a calm interaction in which both of you are listening to each other. The entire process begins with your staying in control as both a participant and an observer and being able to call a time-out at just the right moment if the argument threatens to escalate past the point of no return.

Important: The way of arguing that I describe here is based on the Domestic Violence Safety Plan that is used by all organizations that work with violent couples, so it is the safest way to help couples argue. The time-outs are a safety mechanism and are designed to avoid violence, but if you are in a situation where you are being controlled by abuse, fear of violence, or actual violence, then it is vital that you seek professional help immediately. Domestic violence is illegal, potentially life-threatening, and should be taken very seriously. The exercises in this session are only for women who have communication problems with their boyfriends rather than those who are in dangerous relationships.

Defuse the Fight

Most women I've worked with find it very difficult at first to keep a grip on the situation. They discover themselves being sucked into the destructive spiral of the argument, and so, over the years, I have used a special technique that will help you stay in control and enable you to declare a time-out in order to carry on the exercise effectively.

The secret is to pick a code word to say to yourself, which will be your signal to detach from the argument when you sense that it is headed for real trouble. Here is how it works.

Keep a watch out for when you feel the argument is getting too nasty, wildly irrational, or overly emotional. At that point, recite to yourself the code word you've selected. That is your alarm bell telling you to excuse yourself from the room. Any word will do. Your code word is said, under your breath, before it all goes haywire, whether he is about to lose it or you are. It works both ways. (If he loses it and leaves the room, use the lessons you learned about withdrawal in session 4.) Saying the code word lifts you away from the heat of the moment and lets you become an objective observer of the argument. From this standpoint, you can more easily be aware of how and when the argument gets out of hand.

My code word is "lettuce," because, for me, it breaks the tension in a humorous way and makes me smile a little, which also brings my temperature down a bit. Use my code word, if you like. When you recognize that the argument is taking a nosedive, first identify the words that are leading up to the crash and then simply say to yourself: lettuce.

I expect that your man will be extremely clever about pushing your buttons. Most of them are. He'll know how to get you to the boiling point faster than you might be able to monitor the argument and so forfeit the moment to recite your code word and get back in control. Remember to be patient with yourself.

I fully expect that in the beginning, you will find it difficult to maintain your oasis of objectivity. Yet with each effort, you'll get a firmer grasp of how to stay in charge until you're in control of the tone and the temperature of the argument.

Sounds easy, but believe me, I know it isn't. I fully expect that the first few times you try this, you will totally forget about the book, the exercise, and your code word. But don't fret. You're doing fine, because you are learning to observe your argument, monitor yourself, and identify the moment when you need to disconnect from the fray, using your code word.

Emotionally, it is natural that you want him to cave in, offer an apology, and promise never to act badly again. But he's fed you that line before, and you are smart enough to recognize that going down this path only leads to a short-lived and hollow victory. You know better than anyone how quickly he'll revert back to his old ways. In a matter of days, he'll be behaving badly and pressing your emotional buttons as if nothing has changed. Because it hasn't!

What you deserve is a resolution of the conflicts in your relationship to occur at a higher, more sustainable level; don't settle for a half-felt apology or an empty promise that he'll behave better in the future. Your real "win"—which you will achieve single-handedly—is that, at last, you are now able to discuss what you want in the relationship and prepare the way to get your emotional needs met.

This will work. Because the pattern of your relationship has changed, your intimacy will grow, your communication will improve, and your connection will be strengthened. You now have a framework that puts you in control of disagreements and of getting what you want. You are the referee, calling the shots, crying foul, and observing the game play, safely from the sidelines. And you have done all of this without his knowing participation.

How to Fight: The Aftermath

You've made enormous progress, and you should feel justifiably proud of yourself, but there is a bit more work to do. You need to take one last step in this process. Without your completing this step, the progress you've worked so hard to achieve in your relationship will be temporary. You will find yourself knocked back into the same unhappy corner by his selfish and distancing behavior, leaving you, yet again, shouting, tearful, and spitting mad.

This last step will give you the tools you require to permanently break the cycle of frustration, fear, or disappointment that is the real driver behind every argument. This last exercise will help you discover the deeper message that your repetitive arguments are trying to reveal to you. Once you've heard it, you'll be free to steer your relationship in the direction of your choosing.

• •

Open Your Notebook

To help you complete this lesson, you'll need your notebook. At the end of each argument, jot down a quick snippet describing what it was about. You might want to make a note of whether you needed a code word and if you were successful in using it. Don't write anything elaborate or particularly detailed: "We fought about doing the dishes." Or, "We argued about his comment that I need to go on a diet." Next, recall the lens sentence you formulated back in session 3. Write your lens sentence underneath the description of your argument.

At the end of the lesson, review the weeklong set of arguments in context with your lens statement. Do you see a connection? Could it be that all of your arguments and fights are different variations and expressions of the same fear that you've represented in your lens statement?

Let's revisit the couple we met earlier, in scenario 1. Megan was furious when she was left out of the conversation that Josh was having at the restaurant with his old friend. If she were following the exercises in this session and looking through her notebook at the argument topics for the week, she might read: "He stayed at work late again." "Caught him texting his ex." "Up all night playing his computer games." At first glance, it might not appear that these three instances have much in common, other than maybe she's got legitimate (or not-so-legitimate) grievances. Yet the connection these three events have in common, and the reason she is willing to have a fight about them, is made clear by her lens statement: "I am afraid of being excluded."

In the case of Josh's contacting his ex-girlfriend, it's more than the simple fear that he might be starting things up again with her. Megan has the added deep-seated, primal fear that she'll be pushed out and left all alone. His working late and playing video games are other examples that trigger her fear of being excluded. A woman can be excluded just as easily by activities as by other people. Megan feels cast aside, being forced to share him with activities he is compelled to do (work) and wants to do (play video games).

• •

What Are Your Arguments Really About?

Remember back in session 3 when we discovered the link between fundamental childhood feelings and the way your guy makes you feel? I am certain that the dynamics behind your lens sentences are also being played out in the arguments you have with your partner.

Trina's Tips for Arguing Safely

- Identify an incident in which your partner exhibited an example of the insensitive behavior you want him to change.
- Formulate your XYZ sentence: "When you did X, it made me feel Y; would you please do Z instead?"
- Confront him with his behavior, no holds barred. But observe the argument; keep a part of yourself unengaged and monitor the argument.
- When you sense that you or your boyfriend is about to close in on the point of no return, recite your code word to yourself. Announce that you feel that you need to go into another room for a brief cooling-off period, after which time you'll return to the discussion.
- You may need to go into another room or leave the house entirely. If your argument is especially aggressive, you need to think about how you will be able to leave safely. If you have children, you should be sure they are being cared for by a relative or a friend, if necessary.
- While you are in separate rooms, think about the verbal exchange that triggered the outburst that brought the argument to the boiling point. What did he say? What did you say?

His actions—whether they are premeditated or not—evoke the unhappy, insecure, or fearful moments you experienced long ago. Those feelings that you've packed away in the back of your psychic closet have momentarily been set free by some thoughtless act of your partner and are wreaking havoc with your feelings and your relationship.

It is entirely legitimate for you to want to feel secure, appreciated, or special. It is entirely within your rights to feel protected, popular,

- Go find your boyfriend and see whether he has calmed down and is ready to continue. If he is, then tell him what you think you said or did that contributed to the escalation of the argument. Let the discussion between the two of you start again.

- If he has not calmed down, tell him you are going to be in the next room and will check back later. This is the most difficult part to manage! The separation can be minutes, hours, or days. The length of time is however long it takes for the two of you to calm down and think of your contribution to the argument. If I were seeing both of you in my therapy practice, then he would also be thinking of his contribution to the argument. Right now, however, you have to do the work, which is fine, because you are getting results. I would not be at all surprised if, after a day or two of seeing how you handle your arguments, he begins to consider his contribution to the quarrel, too!

- It is very important that you always come back to continue the argument, so that the issue is not swept under the carpet.

- Repeat this process for as long as it takes to move the conversation from being an argument to an honest exchange of feelings without rancor and without revenge.

or treasured. Never, ever back down from insisting that you receive the very basic and essential emotional requirements you deserve. By understanding how your lens sentence forms the emotional underpinnings of the arguments you've been having with your partner, you will have a deeper understanding on the basic requirements you demand of a fulfilled, secure, and intimate relationship.

The cycle that was established in childhood and that played itself out in every relationship you've ever had is now broken. You are able to rewrite the script of your life as the adult you are now. You are equipped to enter into a relationship of collaborative intimacy that you've made possible entirely without his knowledge—on an equal footing, able to communicate in a shared spirit of cooperation. In this new way of relating, your man will also change how he acts with you.

It's a liberating feeling, isn't it? Because the choice is yours. Being aware of the connection between your deep emotional needs and the source of your arguments with your partner puts you in control of taking the relationship to the next level. No longer are you a puppet on a string, manipulated by buried emotional desires, flailing about in search of some unidentified longing for security or love that your guy constantly denies you.

By understanding which emotional needs must be fulfilled for you to have a successful, satisfied relationship, you can now act in a more self-aware fashion. By using your lens sentence and communicating with XYZ sentences, you can make real progress in getting your guy to stay calm and attentive in the argument without withdrawing; to listen, appreciate you more, understand how you feel, and, hopefully, get on your wavelength so that he agrees to modify his behavior.

Or you can recognize what is happening on a deeper plane of feelings and not let yourself be subjected to the same degree of emotional push and pull when he does something that violates your lens statement. The man you are with may or may not be able to satisfy your most basic and fundamental relationship requirements. But now you are able to ascertain his ability to do so without being overcome by the fog of emotion. You should be proud that you have mastered one of the most challenging skills in life by controlling how you and your partner argue. Reward yourself by selecting the next gift or activity on your list. You've earned your second Communication badge. Relish it. Delight in it. You deserve it. What you do with this power and knowledge is up to you. You are calm, effective, and in control of the relationship.

Don't for a moment think you will ever live a struggle-free life. As I said at the beginning of the session, struggle is the stuff relationships are made of. It is the lifeblood of a healthy union. You may not get your way all the time. You may still disagree about who takes out the garbage on the weekends or what constitutes an appropriate Valentine's Day gift. But now you'll be heard and understood by your man. Before, everything said in the heat of an argument was like a punch to the gut. Now, you've created an unemotional environment where communication is possible. You have opened up the possibility of having a rewarding and mature relationship where your man will understand your point of view. You are living in a collaborative, instead of combative, relationship, in which he is able to provide you with the warm and cozy feeling of a new, deeper level of intimacy.

Isn't that what you really wanted from him all along?

Share Your Roles in the Relationship

Have you ever noticed that when you meet a couple for the first time, your initial impression of them is usually right on target? It is as if the dynamics of their relationship are on display for everyone to see the moment they start to interact with each other:

> She's Ms. Nervous, fidgeting with her jewelry and eyeing the exit for a quick getaway. He's Mr. Cool, showing little or no emotion, acting as if nothing could possibly ruffle him, exuding an air of self-confidence, and staying aloof and detached.

> She's the Neatnik, always in motion, bustling about, puffing up and arranging the pillows on the sofa, making sure the household routine runs on schedule, alphabetizing the monthly bills, and organizing the monthly budget. He's the Slob, slightly scruffy all the time, misplacing his house keys and losing his wallet, forgetting to empty the garbage, and always late for appointments.

She's the Giver, volunteering for worthy causes, visiting sick relatives with homemade cookies, always at home to walk the dog and up early to get her partner to work on time. He's the Taker, the family revolves around his schedule, he's in charge of the TV's remote control, and he expects loads of sympathy whenever he has a mild cold.

You might have noticed this division of roles in the relationships on *Tool Academy*. The couples seem to be acting out their characters almost from the moment they start talking. Nag or stoic, manipulator or victim, antagonist or innocent, it is as if each member of the relationship were performing in a play, speaking dialogue and displaying attitudes patterned on scripted characters.

Many of the women I've helped in the course of therapy believe themselves to be typecast in their relationships. At some level, they feel as if they are acting out characters who do not fully represent their true sense of themselves. These sets of prescribed behaviors imprison them, and the women feel trapped, suffocated, or strait-jacketed. They are unable to give full expression to a wide range of feelings and behaviors, because doing so is somehow not allowed or makes them too uncomfortable.

This session will help you break free of the role-playing constraints that have you bound and gagged, forcing you to act out behaviors that you don't feel all that good about and don't get you what you want. You are going to surreptitiously alter your partner's behavior as well. You have read enough of the book to know that you and your partner, consciously and unconsciously, conspire to keep what you want in the relationship just out of reach. So it shouldn't come as a complete surprise that you and your partner also play a role in creating the drama you feel forced to take part in. In this session, you'll learn how to secretly control his behavior and also to freely express your full range of emotions.

Your Tool Kit So Far

You have come a long way toward achieving what you want in your relationship and understanding how to get it. You know that the key is to peel back layers of attitudes and behaviors that were formed many, many years ago and take control of them, instead of letting them control you.

That's what you did in session 4, to create more intimacy in your relationship. You learned how to control the dynamics of the relationship, in order to create a balance between your emotional needs and those of your partner, at any given moment. You understood how you were not getting the intimacy you wanted, because your lens sentence was being manipulated, your buttons pushed, your string dropped. With this knowledge, you went on to create an environment that was safe for him to express his desire for intimacy, without distancing himself and hiding out in his cave. You learned how to use your understanding of your relationship's string to pull him closer to you, coaxing him into taking on some Pursuer behaviors and apply them toward you.

Give and Take

In this session, we'll extend those underlying concepts beyond intimacy to help you express the range of feelings and behaviors you have previously denied yourself. That's because in the same way that you have learned that you and your partner are both Pursuer and Distancer and that the key to intimacy is sharing these roles appropriately, you will now be introduced to the notion that you and your partner are both Neatniks and Slobs, Givers and Takers, Nervous and Cool. For you to become more emotionally fulfilled and bring the relationship into greater harmony, you will discover how to share with your partner some of the unpleasant behaviors and feelings you are burdened with, and you will take back some of the emotions and behaviors that you've bestowed solely on him.

I'm guessing that you already know what I'm talking about. How can any relationship not feel like a straitjacket if you are allowed to express only limited behaviors? Furthermore, many women tell me that their being restricted to a small subset of emotions also has the effect of making them feel emotionally isolated from other parts of their personalities. They feel that they are living out only a portion of their true identities. They don't have the courage to step outside the prescribed roles they inhabit and don't feel free to explore entire continents of their individuality that they have suppressed but that are hiding just under the surface.

If you and I were talking together, I'm sure you would soon discover that one reason you're acting on a limited set of emotions is that's what you expect of yourself. Yet as you probe more deeply, I believe you'd also learn that not only are these behaviors self-imposed, they are also expected of you by your partner.

Now entertain for just a moment the idea that your partner is in the same predicament as you. He feels himself unable to step outside the circle of a set of behaviors that you expect of him and that he demands of himself. Imagine that your relationship is a globe and your set of acceptable emotions and behaviors is frozen at one pole, while your partner's set is frozen at the opposite pole.

Maybe his set of roles includes doing lots of different sports, always looking at the glass as being half-empty, and taking adventure vacations. Maybe your set includes leading a book club, always looking at the glass as being half-full, and taking stay-at-home vacations. For a long time now you've wanted to take up surfing, but somehow the role you have assigned yourself cannot abide any such thing. So you feel stuck, angry, and cheated.

Let's take a closer look. One of the more common displays of split or divided role playing in a relationship is the Introvert and the Extrovert. You know the types. The Introvert is quiet, shy, withdrawn, and speaks only when spoken to. She stands in the back row for the family photo so that she can't be clearly seen. She wears "quiet" clothing, no loud colors or suggestive styles. On the other hand, the Extrovert takes charge of every conversation, is a bit of a show-off, does everything in an oversized way, and is always the life of the party.

To an outsider, these two may seem like very different and distinct people. But in my experience, the Introvert and the Extrovert possess many of the same qualities. In fact, inside the relationship there is a tangled mess of emotions, many of which they unknowingly share.

What's Yours and What's His?

Let me introduce you to Lela and Sean. Lela, the Introvert, liked intimate dinner parties instead of large group gatherings and took pains to create a neat and orderly home. She cultivated a close group of friends and smiled quietly more often than she laughed out loud. Her idea of a fun night was to rent a movie and watch it on the sofa in the living room, rather than go out to the theater to see a film. As you might expect, Lela shunned bright clothes and stuck to a wardrobe of jeans and beige and brown tops. She was an attractive young woman, but I couldn't help notice that she neglected to comb and even wash her hair and that she avoided makeup, suppressing her natural good looks.

Alternatively, Sean, the Extrovert, displayed many of the polar opposite behaviors and emotions from Lela. Sitting together on my sofa, they looked like they came from different worlds. He strutted into my office first, followed by Lela, who trailed him like his shadow. He was a sharp dresser, always in a shirt with a freshly starched collar, sitting casually with his leg crossed over his knee, unfazed and totally composed. Sean liked nothing better than going out to bars on a Saturday night with a group of his friends. He loved having his picture taken and never passed up an opportunity to entertain his coworkers with a repertoire of jokes. The clothes Sean wore, as well as his body language, also communicated his outgoing personality.

He was an excellent mimic and in conversation would energetically assume the voices and mannerisms of the people he described.

Early in their relationship, Lela and Sean made an unconscious agreement to divide their emotional universe between them, separating it into "his" and "hers." She agreed to be shy, reclusive, timid, and hesitant. He agreed to all of the bold, audacious, assertive, gregarious, outgoing behaviors.

Sean and Lela may seem as if they are utterly opposite and impossibly matched, but in reality they are more similar than they might appear to an outside observer. Remember when I said that the old adage that opposites attract is not really true? Remember also that partners tend to share the same lens sentence. Individuals who share many of the same fears and insecurities usually end up as couples. Sean's Extrovert behavior attracted Lela, because he exuded the confidence and ease that she inherently felt she lacked. And for a long time, she delighted in the many manifestations of his outgoing personality. She allowed him to have a monopoly on gregarious behavior and sole ownership of outwardly expressive emotions.

Sean, on the other hand, was attracted to Lela's demure and unobtrusive style. Everything about the way she dressed and acted seemed to him to convey her intelligence, self-assurance, independence, and self-reliance, all of the qualities he felt he lacked. When they came to see me, they both complained that they wanted "something more" out of the relationship, that it was at "a dead end." They discovered over the successive weeks that they felt this way not because they were with the wrong partner, but because they each felt hemmed in by the roles they were playing in the relationship.

At the beginning of the relationship, Lela could have reserved a bit of outgoing behavior for herself. She had often entertained the idea of taking up singing or joining an amateur theater group but had put those aspirations on hold. She was waiting for an opportunity to come her way when she would feel more comfortable pursuing these goals. Now, eighteen months into the relationship, she felt as if she'd like to give it a try, but she complained to me that she felt that Sean prevented her from trying those activities, and she resented him for it. She was ready to abandon the relationship because, each time she brought up the topic, he made her feel inadequate and put her down.

Many couples face this kind of emotional stagnation. It originates early in the relationship when the couple's romantic attraction and desire for each other are heavily influenced by each partner's role in complementing and protecting the other's lens sentence. Lela defined herself (with her partner's unconscious support) as the one in the relationship who was hesitant and retiring, the one who shunned big groups and open displays of affection. That role worked for her—after all, it reinforced her desire to be accepted, and her strategy was to act in the least offensive or noticeable way possible to avoid censure. It also worked for Sean, who interpreted her calmness and loner qualities to be an inherent sense of inner strength and assurance, which they were.

Your (Paint) Bucket List

The relationship escalated into crisis mode when each member wanted to dip a brush into the other's paint bucket of emotions and behaviors. Let's imagine, if you will, that each emotion and behavior is contained in its own bucket. The relationship began with Lela filling up her buckets and Sean filling up his. She got the "demure" and "shy" bucket, which she filled to the brim. Sean got the "outgoing" and "demonstrative" bucket, which he also filled to the brim. Now Lela is feeling like she wants a bit of what's in Sean's "outgoing" bucket, as well as in the one that is labeled "wild and crazy."

The same is true from Sean's perspective. He'd like nothing better than to allow himself to borrow from Lela's "introspective" bucket every now and again. But that bucket is practically overflowing and is under Lela's control. Take a moment to consider your relationship.

There is probably a whole palette of emotions and behaviors you'd love to experiment with, to dip your brush into, and paint a new and vibrant portrait of yourself and your relationship. But first, you'll have to find a way to acquire some of the colors from the buckets that are in your partner's custody. And to do that, you'll need to better understand how the buckets got to be divided in the first place, and this requires you to review your lens sentence.

Apply Your Lens Sentence

Perhaps your lens sentence is about your fear of being alone, your anxiety about being labeled a failure, or a dread of being inadequate. In previous sessions, you've worked through the genesis of those feelings. Did your mother care for a stepfather and abandon her responsibilities toward you? Did you live your life in the shadow of your sister because she was the "gifted and talented" sibling? Did your father so desperately want a son that he took every opportunity to let you know he was disappointed with having a daughter? Every one of us has a unique lens sentence and set of circumstances that created it. Let's take a closer look at how our lens sentences influence the way we distribute the contents of our emotional and behavioral buckets.

As we have seen, Lela's strategy to gain acceptance was to avoid any opportunity to distinguish herself in any way. Lela's lens sentence ("I am afraid of being criticized") originated when, as a young girl, her mother and father disapproved of her. Lela was the fourth child of a financially strapped family, and her parents really hadn't wanted to have another child. Lela never got close to her sisters, because they were so much older. Lela's parents referred to her as the "accident" and criticized her looks, her clothes, her grades, and her friends. One particularly searing memory that she repeated on several occasions was being reduced to tears at the age of eight by her father, who flew into a rage when she stuck a stamp upside down on his phone bill. All of this verbal abuse took its toll. Lela avoided any and all activities that might attract positive or negative attention to herself. She went to extraordinary lengths to avoid resentment, envy, or rebuke from her parents or anyone else.

Lela's need to avoid criticism was instrumental in terms of attracting—and being attracted to—a partner. She was naturally drawn to a man who seemed to embrace the limelight, someone who enjoyed receiving attention in all of its many forms and who craved recognition. Because she hated the idea of being put on a pedestal of any kind, who better to hook up with than a guy who drew the attention away from her? In this way, she could safely inhabit the role in which she was most comfortable.

Sean's lens sentence also described a fear of criticism, disapproval, and condemnation, so from his perspective Lela was the perfect fit. Sean and Lela shared several important family traits, although they came from quite different backgrounds. Sean's father was in the military, and as an only child, Sean was held up to a set of very high and sometimes impossible expectations. When Sean didn't excel in sports or academics, his father severely chastised him. In addition, Sean's father often withheld praise when it was deserved or dispensed it very sparingly. By selecting Lela as his partner, Sean could be assured that he would be the "star" of the relationship and have every opportunity to shine.

The styles of behavior that Sean and Lela adopted to cope with their mutual fear of disapproval were very different. For Lela, it meant melting into the scenery and being as invisible as possible. For Sean, it was trying to be as likable and affable as possible. In order not to trigger his lens sentence, Sean wanted to get rid of any feeling he had of being mediocre, second-rate, and ordinary. Lela, too, needed to offload any possibility of feeling inadequate, so as not to activate her lens sentence. Like two strips of Velcro, Sean possessed an aversion to being average and Lela abhorred distinguishing herself. His avoidance of all-things-average stuck to Lela's receptivity to all-things-ordinary, and vice versa.

Let's Make a Deal!

It's clear that Lela's introverted behavior and Sean's extroverted behavior are linked to each other in a deep and binding way. Early in their relationship they made a deal, and it was this: Lela would take those buckets of emotion and behaviors that involved being withdrawn and reserved, while Sean would take ownership of the buckets that held the sociable and outgoing behaviors. Nothing was agreed to in any overt or obvious way. It was a pact they made unconsciously, so that each had his or her own set of behaviors. Borrowing from each other was off limits, lest the partner feel threatened and the relationship's boundaries be trespassed.

This kind of deal can be found in most relationships. At the beginning of the relationship, the roles assumed by the partners usually work quite well, until one of the partners begins to grow tired of the same old, same old and yearns for something more. The hard part is knowing how to step out of your character, because not only have you put yourself in that role, but you have also been quite comfortable assuming it. Add to the mix that your partner is also very secure with your role (and his!), and any attempts to change it will be perceived with anxiety and met with resistance.

You are both invested in displaying behavior that the other wishes to avoid, so that in order to change some of your roles, you'll need to decide which ones you want to keep, which ones you want to have less of, and, to begin with, which ones are the easiest to work on. Once you manage that, you'll be able give your man some of the contents of your bucket so that you're not carrying all of its weight, and you'll be able to take back some of the behaviors and emotions that are in his buckets and make them your own.

Allow Yourself a Full Range of Emotions

Here's an exercise that will help you distinguish some of the emotions and behaviors you have unconsciously unloaded on your partner and identify others that you want to allow yourself to express.

EXERCISE

Ten Things I Hate about Myself

List ten things you do in your relationship that cause you to be upset with yourself. Think about situations and behaviors that you often scold yourself about afterward. Do you dislike yourself for being the nag when your partner neglects to tidy up after himself? Do you get angry with yourself for feeling a flicker of envy when he goes out with his pals to the bar? Do you hate yourself for lying to him about where you've been whenever you go shopping with your girlfriends?

Review your lens sentence to assist you in this task. It contains clues to help you locate some of the feelings and behaviors that you dislike about yourself. For example, if your lens sentence reads something like, "I am afraid of being out of control," then you can write down all of the feelings and reactions that would help you stay in control, but that also make you hate yourself for being controlling.

This list will prompt you to think about certain behaviors and feelings that make you uncomfortable:

1. Being angry
2. Feeling inadequate
3. Being demanding
4. Always nagging
5. Being envious
6. Constantly lying and being deceptive
7. Feeling shy
8. Doing all of the work

9. Being the adult

10. Always being the caregiver

○ ○ ○

Let's revisit Lela and see how she might complete this exercise. Lela's lens sentence was, "I am afraid of being criticized." Her list of uncomfortable behaviors culled from the previous list could include:

1. Being angry

2. Feeling inadequate

3. Being envious

4. Constantly lying and being deceptive

5. Feeling shy

Remember, this list of behaviors and feelings is a reaction to Lela's acting on her lens sentence. By protecting the feelings that she expressed in her lens sentence and removing herself from any possibility of receiving criticism, she encounters situations that make her feel uncomfortable and unhappy with herself. These are the kinds of items I want you to write down.

For example, let's suppose that Lela is among three colleagues to win the employee of the month award at work. Yet instead of going out with her fellow coworkers for drinks after work, she excuses herself and goes home at the normal time to fix dinner for Sean.

Lela is so fearful of anything that might be the cause of someone's disapproval or displeasure that her immediate reaction is "she is not worthy of the award" (feeling inadequate). When called on to say a few words in public, she can "barely speak" (shy) and wishes she knew how the other employees were able to casually make jokes as they "accept their awards" (envy). When asked why she won't join the after-work celebration, she invents the "excuse of having a doctor's appointment" (lying and being deceptive). On the drive home, she is "so angry with herself" that she goes through a red light and practically gets into an accident (anger).

Now that we know Lela a little better, let's see what other five items might be on Lela's list:

6. Not speaking up for myself

7. Having to perform all of the daily household chores

8. Having others always rely on me

9. Letting others always go first

10. Always berating myself about how I could have acted differently

It is clear that Lela's sense of who she is prevented her from saying a few words of thanks in public, calling up Sean and telling him she wasn't coming home for dinner, and going out for a drink with her office buddies. Part of the reason lies in her own self-imposed barriers. Such behavior would have activated her lens sentence: "I'm afraid of being criticized."

But another reason she withdrew from the celebration was that socializing and entertaining of any kind belonged in Sean's territory. Lela didn't have a bucket for "partying" because she had given hers to Sean, which he was only too happy to fill to the brim. But every now and then, she wanted to take "partying" back. With Lela's example in mind, review your list and ask yourself, "What emotional and behavioral buckets have I given away to my partner?" If you've written "Having to pick up after him," ask yourself whether you have assigned him the "messiness" bucket. If you've written "Having to balance the family checkbook," ask yourself whether you have given him the "free of financial responsibility" bucket. And if you've written on your list things that make you uncomfortable, such as "Always going to his parents' house for holidays and birthdays," then ask yourself whether you've given him the "party planner" bucket. As difficult and complex as it is to comb through all of the behaviors and feelings you avoid and dump on him, what makes this process doubly hard and complicated is that your partner is also unloading on you buckets of behaviors and feelings that he wants to avoid. It's not an easy task to distribute your roles more evenly, because you will have to take back the uncomfortable feelings you listed previously—all of the ones that activate your lens sentence. This is why I want you to be selective and only work on the buckets that you're happy to dip into.

Once again, if you want to change what you are getting out of the relationship, you'll need to understand how and why you—and your partner—behave in context to each other. By having a better understanding of the relationship script you have written, with him in a starring role, you'll have more opportunities to change the script and your role, to fulfill more of your needs and desires.

Many of the women I see in my practice believe that rekindling the romance of the relationship until the flame is as hot as it was in the beginning would solve all of their relationship woes. To put it bluntly, nothing could be further from the truth. Even if it were possible to turn back the clock, there was much more than romance going on beneath the surface during those first few weeks and months of courtship than either of you was aware of. The work you did with your genogram and lens sentence has given you an idea of the many forces at work in your relationship, including those at the beginning. These forces also play a role in dividing which emotions and behaviors go into the "his" and "her" buckets.

Your Invisible Deal

Let's peek at what your mind-set was like at the beginning of your relationship, which helped shape the trajectory of your love life as you are living it today. The following questions, devised by a colleague of mine, will help you start to think about the emotional deal you struck with your man when you first met him.

Your Invisible Deal

The following questions will help you explore the unconscious deal you and your man made in the relationship. Take your time, be honest, and use the knowledge you gained from previous sessions to help you with the answers.

1. What was it that your partner was meant to provide for you? For example:

   Did you think he would provide you with emotional or financial security? Did he make you feel more like a woman than any man you'd ever been with? Did he make you laugh out loud and forget all of your troubles? Did you hope his flair and sense of adventure would rescue you from a dull and boring existence?

2. How was your partner going to "heal" you? For example:

   Was your partner going to satisfy your aching need for the love and affection you felt was missing from previous relationships? Would his compliments help bolster your self-confidence and self-assurance? Did his belief in your talent, skill, and intelligence give you the courage to take your career to the next level? Did you believe that his constant attention to you would remedy your feelings of being unattractive and undesirable?

3. What was your partner supposed to be so that you'd feel better about yourself? For example:

   A steady provider? Loyal and respectful? Confident and self-assured? Loving and attentive? A male version of you?

4. What behaviors did your partner act out, so that you wouldn't have to, that angered or annoyed you? For example:

   Worrying about your clothes, looks, and body? Always horny? Excessively competitive? Always hungry?

Smoking cigarettes? Drinking too much? Talking back to the boss at work? Always late? Acting stupid? Texting at the dinner table?

In my experience, clients who answer these questions become sensitized to the hidden expectations they had of their partners from the very beginning of the relationship, when the romantic and sexual feelings were so supercharged that they clouded any other perspective. Remember that your partner is completely unaware of the expectations you have of him. He hasn't the slightest notion of the role you've assigned him to play in your relationship. Is it any wonder that he disappoints you as often as he does?

○ ○ ○

Let's look at Lela's questionnaire and see what she wrote about her relationship with Sean.

What was it that your partner was meant to provide for you?

I wanted him to provide me with the safety and security that I realize I never managed to achieve in any of the other relationships I've had. He was supposed to give me the approval and support I always felt was missing. I wanted him to shelter me from all of the harshness and unfairness in the world.

How was your partner going to "heal" you?

He was going to make me feel taken care of and would love me no matter how frightened or awkward I felt. He was going to make me feel feminine and desirable. His love would help me overcome all petty jealousies and criticism.

What was your partner supposed to be, so that you'd feel better about yourself?

Nurturing. Strong but supportive like my father. Independent and totally self-assured.

What behaviors did your partner act out, so that you wouldn't have to, that angered or annoyed you?

The way he attracts attention from everyone in the room. He's so flashy. He thinks he is so great at work and brags about his achievements all the time.

Lela's answers hold some interesting insights, particularly as they pertain to the emotional and behavioral buckets I've been discussing. When I first saw Lela in my practice, she came across as someone who couldn't care less what other people thought of her. She was totally resistant to the office gossip and the petty backbiting that occurs in the workplace. She was soft-spoken and chose her words carefully. The way she dressed and spoke almost dared anyone to approach her, much less try to befriend her.

My guess was there was much more beneath the surface, and reading her questionnaire reaffirmed my hunch. In her bid to protect her lens sentence ("I am afraid of criticism") and unload onto her partner many of the qualities she loathed about herself, Lela now found herself trapped in a role she no longer wanted to play, with a partner who was oblivious to her expectations, who repeatedly either annoyed or disappointed her.

She was quietly furious at him, at herself, at her family, at the world—but because anger was one of "his" buckets, even that emotional outlet was inaccessible to her.

Women who have closed themselves off from being able to express their justifiable and natural feelings of anger and frustration leave themselves few options. Their volatile feelings build up over the months and years until something inside them just snaps. They can become violent toward others or themselves, behave irrationally, or descend into a certifiable clinical depression. That is why it is so very important to safely release yourself from the stereotypes of expected behavior, in order to restore emotional balance, in yourself and in your relationship.

Break Free of Constricting Roles

Get ready to step into uncharted territory. I am going to ask you to begin by raiding one of your boyfriend's buckets of behavior. That's right. You will act out a role that is usually assigned to him. It will seem very strange at first, even a bit dangerous and risky, but this feeling will not last for long. All change feels disorienting and uncomfortable at the start, which is why we stick to what we know and play it safe. But if you maintain a little self-discipline, you will be able to determine your true feelings and separate them from the ones your partner has thrust on you. As the emotional tangle of your relationship begins to straighten out, you will be able to control when, where, and how you express yourself.

The following exercise will help you break free from constricting and confining roles.

EXERCISE

The Container Exercise

The following two lists contain roles found in most relationships. They are not meant to be exhaustive, so as you work through the exercise, feel free to add items to either or both lists.

Things You Do

Caretaker/Patient

Planner/Spontaneous Drifter

Mother/Child

Overachiever/Lazy

Saver/Spender

Tidy/Messy

Things You Feel

Angry/Even-tempered

Domineering/Submissive

Optimistic/Pessimistic

Outgoing/Timid

Sexy/Conservative

Worrier/Happy-go-lucky

The first step is to choose and write in your notebook those items that you feel best describe you and your relationship. Take a look at the "Things You Do" list. If you feel as if you are always taking physical and emotional care of a needy partner, choose "Caretaker/Patient" and "Mother/Child." If you are always picking up after him and cleaning up the dishes every night, choose "Tidy/Messy." And if you are the one who keeps tabs on the family budget, while he blows the gas money on tickets to the football game, then choose "Saver/Spender."

Next, review the categories listed under "Things You Feel." When, for example, you find yourself stuck in traffic and late for an engagement, are you the one being patient, while he curses and pounds the steering wheel with his fist? Then you should choose "Angry/Even-tempered." When you are planning a vacation, is he the one who dictates when you travel, what you do, and where you stay? If this situation sounds familiar and frequent, then choose Domineering/Submissive.

Putting the Container Exercise into Action

Here comes the fun part! Select one of the "doing" traits you've checked that you particularly want to gain control of and that is also the trait you think will be easiest to work on. If you have identified that you are a planner, a mother, and a perfectionist, then the next time he relies on you to organize a family party, plan a vacation, clean his closet, or take the car in to get the oil changed, I want you to follow a very simple instruction: don't! Avoid doing any of these things. Make excuses not to get the chore done. Steer clear of the activity he depends on you to do. By not performing the role that is expected of you, you will be gently but firmly refusing to let him off-load the activities (and the emotions) he doesn't feel comfortable with.

Let's suppose that your most obvious "doing" trait is overachiever, while his is being just plain lazy. You do everything. You clean, cook, organize, and take responsibility for the finances, the repairs for the car, and getting the furnace fixed—everything. It's as if you're the adult and he's the child. So the next time you both come home from a long day at work and the two of you sit on the sofa in front of the TV, and he nudges you and says, "What's for dinner, babe?" I want you to stop yourself from responding in what has been your answer for weeks, months, and even years. After all, you've had a hard day, too. It's infuriating the way he expects you to simply conjure up dinner and place it on the table, night after night. Something is different this time. You now recognize that you are performing an activity that fills up the bucket you've labeled "overachiever."

So instead of saying something like, "I'll look in the fridge," or "It'll be ready in a half hour" and trotting off into the kitchen, simply respond in a sweet, innocent tone, "I have no idea, babe." Stay engrossed in watching TV. Stick it out and see what he does next. He may try to good-naturedly coax you into making dinner or may get impatient with you, but I want you to turn the situation around and act lazy, tired, as if you couldn't be bothered. Yawn. Stretch out as if you are going to be on the sofa all night. But don't give in. Even if you're hungry, it will be worth it to tough it out now for the rewards that will come your way.

I guarantee that—sooner or later—he will be in the kitchen fixing himself something to eat, even if it is only a sandwich for himself. Remember, this exercise isn't about who cooks dinner. In this example, it is about your taking on all of the caregiving in the relationship and being the over-doer. This time you are letting him share some of the caring, allowing him to be the adult and to use some energy to take care of himself.

It would be absurd to think that he will suddenly start making you three-course meals every night. And you may want to go back to cooking because you are good at it and you like it. But if you repeat this exercise three or four times (or use one that applies to you and your situation), you will have begun to share some of the contents of your "overachiever" bucket with him, and, in return, you will be able to indulge in a bit of what's in his "lazy" bucket.

You may want to try the same approach with some of the other activities that you've assigned to yourself, such as shopping, cleaning, paying the bills, and planning the vacations. Be prepared to wait it out. If your trait is being tidy, you will have to put up with his messiness for a while until he gets the message. He may be upset with you because the house is suddenly a mess. But instead of fighting back or trying to explain yourself, sit back and relax and try to endure a messy house for a while. Act happy-go-lucky or distracted or simply as if you just don't care anymore. Don't tell him to clean up. You've tried that before, and it didn't do much good. Just quietly watch from the sidelines and see him start to take a bit of the responsibility for cleaning the house, picking up the dirty clothes, and doing the dishes.

It's a bit like training a toddler. You are being contrary and acting out the opposite, to get him to pick up his cue and behave differently. As he learns his new role of taking more responsibility for the traits that you are giving back to him, you will be able to gain back some of the elements you have lost in the relationship. He will grow up, become a more mature man, and leave his old ways behind. Can it be that you secretly manipulated your man into assuming the role of a responsible adult?

To give you another example of how powerful this exercise can be, let's revisit Lela and Sean. Lela, as we know, is an introvert, and it probably wouldn't surprise you if I characterized her as someone who is also a bit pessimistic (looks on the negative side of things), uptight (doesn't trust herself to lose control), and even-tempered (doesn't want to give in to her emotions). On Lela's list of "Things You Do," she might have chosen Caregiver/Patient, Saver/Spender, and Tidy/Messy. On the list "Things You Feel," she might have picked Sexy/Conservative and Worrier/Happy-go-lucky. As an introvert, Lela shied away from any activity or expansive behavior that would set her apart or draw attention to her. And Sean, as we know, was the outgoing, carefree, easygoing optimist.

One day, however, Sean came home practically manic with excitement. He had overheard a telephone conversation in which his boss mentioned that there was a sales manager job opening up soon in one of the affiliate stores. Sean couldn't contain himself. Being a hopeless optimist, he was certain that his boss had mentioned the job while Sean was in the room as a hint that he would be considered for the job. Sean became more and more excited, reviewing his work history, remembering all of the compliments he was ever paid on the job, until, after about fifteen minutes of telling Lela the story, he was not only convinced he had the job but was working out how high a salary he should ask for.

Lela saw her opportunity. Having been sensitized to the idea that Sean was putting all of his pessimism and negativity onto her, she let herself dip into his optimism bucket. Lela changed tactics. In the past, she might has responded, "Now hang on, Sean! You know that he likes the other guy at your office better than you, and weren't you saying the other day that you wanted to quit the company altogether?" But instead she managed to say, "Oh, that's terrific. You'd be perfect for that job. And it's closer than the old job, so your commute would be less, too. I can just see the faces of your coworkers when you get called into the front office! They're going to be so jealous. No one deserves it more than you."

Lela held her ground, bubbling with enthusiasm, making plans for what to do with the extra money, figuring out on a calendar when the job might take effect. What happened next surprised even Lela. Sean slowly, but very clearly, began to curb his exuberance.

He didn't become negative about the possibility of a promotion, but instead began to consider the situation in a more balanced and realistic fashion. He pointed out that he'd have to compete with other sales reps, and the job would be posted in the newspaper, so there may be competition from outside the store. Yet the boss recognized his good work. Sean resolved to put in some extra effort now that he knew about the new position.

Lela borrowed just enough of Sean's overconfidence to allow him to be realistic about his chances. And it gave Lela the thrilling opportunity to do something she had wished to do for a long, long time: be positive, hopeful, and constructive.

The Wisdom of Maturity

I want to caution you that there will be some unexpected bumps along the way, and they'll come from unanticipated sources. That's because as you begin to demonstrate behaviors that were formerly your guy's terrain, you'll also leave room for him to take on some of the characteristics that were exclusively yours. You'll suddenly be dealing with a guy who has a fuller range of behaviors, some of which you won't particularly like. If he was passive and did not express anger easily, you will now be living with someone who allows himself to get into a rage and display his anger openly. If your guy was an extravagant spender, wasting his money on unnecessary luxuries, you may find yourself with someone who will occasionally be quite cheap.

Yet consider the upside. You will be able to inhabit your personality more fully and express a broader range of feelings. A new world of emotions and behaviors will open up to you. You can possess all of your emotions, instead of being confined to those he's not comfortable with or that don't fit his perception of himself. You'll have emotionally liberated yourself (and him!) without his knowledge.

You might already be experiencing a few rewards from taking back some of the emotions that you've previously made the exclusive purview of your partner. Many of the women I've helped report a feeling of renewal and broadened horizons. Give yourself a well-deserved pat on the back. Well done! You've accomplished the commendable task of placing your relationship on a stronger, more mature footing.

Consult your list of rewards from your notebook and pick the sixth item you've listed. Indulge yourself with the activity you prescribed for yourself; it is your Maturity badge. By understanding how to control the emotional boundaries between you and your partner, you will be able to enjoy a relationship that is much more satisfying from now on, a relationship that is complete, calm, and balanced.

How to Deal with Your Tool's Cheating

The Fantasy of the Forbidden Fruit

Available and attractive men. All of a sudden, they're everywhere.

At the club, glancing at you in the mirrors when they think you're not noticing. In the office, where you caught that cute exec staring down your blouse as you reached over his desk to pick up a file. And, OMG, when did your boyfriend's brother suddenly get so good-looking? You're sure you are not mistaken that he has been checking you out lately, in that way that makes you feel so sexy.

Where did all of these gorgeous men come from, staring at you as if tasting you from afar and almost daring you to make a move?

There's no denying that you and your partner have been fighting a lot lately. And that you feel lonely and neglected. He's pretty much excluded you from his thoughts and feelings. And sex? Plenty is missing in that department, so let's not go there.

Anyway, who could blame you for thinking about being with another man? So many possibilities. So many opportunities. Maybe you're not even fantasizing about an affair—that might pose too many difficulties, be too complicated. But what about a one-night stand? Several of your girlfriends have had them, and you saw how turned on they got. What about you? Someone just for a night to make you feel the thrill of being desirable and alive again? And besides, that would teach your guy a lesson!

But hold on. Not so fast. All is not lost. You haven't totally given up hope or entirely accepted that your relationship cannot recover. After all, it's not as if you are turned off by your man. He's still number one. If he'd only let you in, be more attentive, make you feel desirable and more like a woman.

Still . . . considering the mood you're in now, with temptation all around, you can't help wondering what it would be like . . .

Who's Cheating?

Most women whose relationships are in crisis fantasize about having an affair. Yet they also confess to feeling torn between their desires and their guilt, their loyalty and their longing. Not only are their fantasies about cheating fairly common, they are entirely natural. I tell women who come to me, confused and tantalized by their desire to have sex outside of the relationship, that their predicament is entirely understandable. When a woman feels powerless and alone, she quite reasonably has an urge to fill her needs elsewhere, by whatever means are available to her. Maybe you already experimented with having sex with someone else and are now dealing with its outcomes and implications. Whether your man has found out already or not, this has probably only made it more difficult for you to stay in the relationship you are trying to salvage.

Most likely, however, because you are reading this book, you are the one who is suspicious that he is cheating on you.

Call it intuition, a woman's sixth sense, or his sudden, odd, and unexplained behavior, but something you can't ignore is telling you that either he had or is currently having an affair with another woman.

Infidelity Smashes a Relationship

There is no way to minimize the emotional toll that infidelity exacts on a relationship, regardless of who is the perpetrator and who is the injured party. It threatens the very foundation on which two people depend if they are to build a life together. The subsequent pain is immeasurable. Trust, self-esteem, respect, and pride are collateral damage in what is one of the most violent—yet recoverable—acts suffered by anyone in a relationship. I say recoverable, because it is entirely possible for a relationship to survive infidelity. It is not an easy process and certainly not a quick one. But if certain crucial positive factors in the relationship survive intact, then a relationship can not only continue, but thrive.

Statistics tell us that six out of ten relationships will have one member cheat on the other. If you have been cheated on or suspect you are currently being betrayed by your lover, this session will help you move through the stages of recovery—assuming one specific condition: that you want to. Only you, after working through the exercises and the advice in this session, will be able to answer that question. Some women have terminated their relationships because after they understood the dynamics of their partners' betrayal, they realized that their men were too undependable, the pain and risk insurmountable, and ultimately the work required to get the relationship back on track was simply not worth the effort. Others felt that with the understanding and control they achieved in therapy, their relationships now had the best chance to grow and provide a sustained sense of purpose, fulfillment, and reciprocated love.

This session is meant to stand independently from the other sessions in this book. You can stay in the stages of reconciliation for as long as you feel necessary, before—or alongside—the other sessions and exercises. Remember, cheating is an emotional trauma to you, your partner, and your relationship. It will take longer than one session for all three to get over an infidelity.

Three Infidelity Types

It might surprise you that although there are infinite variations, only three basic types of infidelity exist. I'll describe them here.

THE THREE-LEGGED STOOL

The first type of infidelity is often called the "three-legged stool." That is because, like a stool, the arrangement between the three individuals (the primary couple and the lover) lends a kind of stability to the entire relationship as a whole. Without the affair, the relationship would be quite wobbly. All of the pressure and tension between the primary couple is absorbed and stabilized by the lover who is the third member in the relationship. These types of relationships usually last for years and have the tacit knowledge of the person being betrayed. This scenario applies to the serial cheater as well, the individual who doesn't have one long-term lover but is always splitting the primary relationship with a continual stream of ongoing cheating.

THE EXIT AFFAIR

The second type of infidelity is the "exit affair." Here, the partner cheats in order to leave the relationship. Many men and women find it too painful to leave their partners without having established a loving, secure relationship to absorb the ordeal of separation.

I will not dwell on these two types of cheating in this session because I am guessing that because you are reading this book and you probably suspect that your partner is cheating on you, you will fall into the third category of infidelity: the communication affair.

THE COMMUNICATION AFFAIR

When a woman discovers that her guy has been cheating on her, her typical response is to explain it away with his need for more, different, or better sex. She blames herself for not providing for her man's sexual needs, thinking that he was driven into the arms of another woman to have his sexual requirements satisfied, or he was led astray by women who continually came on to him. Yet if you listen, as I have, to guys talk about why they cheated on their girl-friends and wives, they mostly confess to deep feelings of insecurity, self-loathing, unworthiness, and fear. What they would say—if only they could—is that their cheating was really a cry for attention. You may not believe it, but when a man cheats, he is pleading to be appreciated in a way that will protect him from feelings associated with his lens sentence. It may seem like a very twisted and imma-ture way to ask for affection and understanding, but nonetheless, that's what it is: a last-ditch attempt to have his emotional—not sexual—needs satisfied.

The juvenile way that men often try to demand the emotional boost they need from you reminds me of a little child who is try-ing to get his mother to notice him while she is busy shopping. He's tugging on her coat, crying, "Mommy, Mommy, Mommy, Mommy," but his mother is distracted by her shopping and is not paying attention. So the little boy grabs a jar off the grocery store shelf and deliberately smashes it on the floor. Now he has her atten-tion! But it's the wrong sort, and, losing her temper, she loudly scolds him and brings him to tears, in the same way that an affair finally smashes the relationship. The disaster is out in the open, and both couples are now forced to focus on the conflict.

Infidelity is not an unsolved mystery. Your guy is trying to com-municate with you. He wants you to listen to him, to pay attention, to provide him with the intimacy he is thirsting for. The irony is, of course, that you also feel the need for intimacy. The problem, as we've seen in sessions 3, 4, and 6, is that while you both want the same thing, you are trying to communicate your mutual needs in entirely different ways. You misinterpret the signals and aren't able to hear each other. This inability to be in sync also drives him to attempt increasingly dangerous behavior, putting the relationship more and more at risk, in order to make a connection. That is why he left lipstick on his collar or put his cell phone where you could find it to read his texts. Unconsciously, he wants you to know. He's dying for you to know. If he's not found out, then his cheating was a waste of time.

One of the classic miscommunications about cheating comes from the very different ideas about how people define it. Couples blithely go through their relationships without ever discussing their definition of cheating. Often, women have a very different notion of cheating than men do. Because a woman's temperament is usually much more protective, motherly, and proprietary, she tends to define cheating more broadly than a man does. And when her man crosses the line—whether it's after-work drinks with a female colleague or a quick kiss-and-hug good-bye with the wife of his friend—the man is often surprised to receive such a strong reaction from his partner. To his way of thinking, it was a bit of innocent flirtation, but to her, he has betrayed a sacred trust. Because you haven't made clear your views on the subject, he unwittingly abides by his rules and definitions of what cheating is and what it isn't.

What Is Infidelity?

If you haven't already done so, it is important to work out your guidelines for what cheating means to you and then have a very candid discussion with your boyfriend, to let him know where you draw the line.

For example, many women are devastated when they discover that their men have been having purely nonphysical relationships with women on the Internet. They feel as violated and betrayed as if their partners had been conducting illicit liaisons in motel rooms with these women. Conversations in Internet chat room relationships can be quite intimate, without ever being physically consummated. A man can spend hours talking to a woman, sharing with her many of his deep personal feelings, feelings his partner believes should be reserved for her and her alone. When the woman discovers her man's virtual infidelity, she feels as crushed as she would if he and the other woman were having physical, instead of verbal, intercourse.

Another Web-based variety of infidelity is watching porn, which has become an increasing source of friction and dissolution of relationships in recent years. Infidelity is usually about "getting something of value from someone or something outside the relationship." As you have noticed, sex is a useful barometer of the relationship; it is usually the first to go and the last to come back when couples are in crisis. Men can often go to porn sites on the Internet to find a release from the sexual frustration that is building up in the relationship. It is sometimes the only "sex" a man is getting. To a woman, it can certainly feel as if he is cheating, although he is all on his own with his computer. It can be a normal and healthy part of your relationship if you are aware of it and happy about it, but it rarely feels acceptable when there are problems in the relationship.

As you begin to think about what constitutes infidelity for you, remember that we defined intimacy in session 4 as the "closest distance possible between you and your partner that enables you to maintain your independence and sense of identity." Cheating factors into this equation, insofar as it can be defined as "any activity that intrudes on you and your partner's ability to be intimate." This means that your partner can be cheating on you with a woman at work or with his buddies who are his first choice when it comes to hanging out in his free time. He can be cheating on you by spending every Saturday night on the Internet or by meeting up with his ex in the evenings when he says he's working late at the office.

Any activity that infringes on a partner's time or ability to engage in meaningful intimate behavior in a relationship can be thought of as cheating. It may not technically be infidelity. No bodily fluids may have been exchanged. But to you, it feels like cheating when your partner is engaged in any kind of activity that robs you of the opportunity to be intimate with him. These are your rules; you know where you draw the line. You will instinctively know what feels okay and what does not.

● ●

Open Your Notebook

With this in mind, open your notebook and make a list of the kind of activities you consider to be cheating. Sex usually heads up the list, and if so, what kind and how much? Is your partner cheating on you if he thinks about another woman while he's making love to you? Is it cheating if he has a close platonic relationship with another woman? Do you feel differently if that woman is his ex? Many women complain that their boyfriends spend more time in the garage tinkering with their cars than they do in the bedroom. Is your man cheating on you with his love of refurbishing old cars? (Remember, I am not saying that your partner should abandon his friends or hobbies for you. A healthy relationship allows for the give-and-take of both partners' interests outside the relationship. It becomes problematic only when those outside interests are used to avoid issues in the relationship or to seek something of value that could be created within the relationship.)

Below are some additional items that you may or may not consider cheating. Copy the list into your notebook, adding more if you need to, and check off the items you feel cross the line into cheating territory. In the column labeled "Him," check off the items that you think he would say is cheating.

Activity	*You*	*Him*
Kissing		
Intimate conversation via phone calls		
Frequent contact with an ex		
Asking women for their phone numbers		
Regular contact with a woman without sexual contact		
Fantasizing about another woman		
Consumer of Internet porn		
Oral sex (on him)		
Oral sex (to another woman)		
Lying		
Meeting people in Internet chat rooms		
Friends with someone on Facebook whom you know your partner disapproves of		
Weekend rehearsals with his band		
Working on his car in the garage in the evenings		
Playing video games		

Look back over your answers and you'll probably notice that although men and women agree that there is a line to be crossed, they disagree on what the line is. It is rare in my experience to find a couple that agrees on what constitutes infidelity.

• •

Are You in Denial?

Women are very good at denial. They suspect that their partners are being unfaithful, yet in some cases even if they have irrefutable evidence, they still can't bring themselves to fully believe it. This is very clearly the case for many of the women on *Tool Academy*. Only when they sit with me in the therapy room does the full meaning of their partners' cheating hit them. It is as if a part of them really doesn't want to know. They are protecting themselves, not only from the painful feelings of betrayal, but also from an internal conflict with themselves. Many women tell themselves categorically that if they ever found out their partners were cheating on them, they would leave the relationships. But now that they suspect their partners are having affairs, their feelings of hurt pride cannot be reconciled with their feelings of love that say "stay." So, to avoid the conflict, they close their eyes until the truth becomes too obvious and unavoidable.

Being betrayed is a searing, emotionally devastating experience. Yet despite the pain and feelings of violation, the road to reconciliation really depends on your ability to take some level of responsibility for what has happened. It feels unjust, I know. After all, you aren't the one who did all of the lying and the deception. He's the one who sneaked around, spent money on another woman, and had sex with her. You were the one left at home, believing he was still at the office. And now you feel like a fool, a victim, and you have a right to your pain and indignation, even a right to punish him and take your revenge, if you want it.

Part of the healing process is to vent these feelings and express them safely. But be careful not to indulge in the feelings excessively or for too long. At some point, you will need to make a decision. You can pack your bags and leave him, or you can choose to rebuild the trust and move forward with the relationship. If you do the latter, then you will need to accept some responsibility for your partner's infidelity. You will need to understand your role in the cheating. It doesn't excuse him for what he did. This simply makes it possible for you to take control of the situation and move it in the direction you want. So the next step you need to take is to understand what he wants to tell you. What is it that you can't hear?

Can You Hear the Truth?

When Lisa visited my office, her life was in shambles. It was obvious from the way she cobbled half sentences together and was unable to follow a single train of thought that she felt as if she just didn't know where to turn to get help for a crumbling relationship. She burst into my office and shut the door firmly behind her as if she had been chased by a pack of angry dogs. I welcomed her, and on hearing my greeting, she collapsed in a chair and let out a deep sigh. Her entire body went slack, as if finally released from an enormous effort to stay in one piece. After she collected herself and became more comfortable, I learned that Lisa had never thought of herself as a particularly suspicious person, but her boyfriend, Tony, had been behaving strangely for months now. In the evenings, he'd slip out to the backyard to take "business" calls but refused to tell her what he was talking about or to whom. Lisa knew something was up, so one night she scrolled through his cell phone and found three flirtatious text messages, each signed Babygirl. Enraged and brokenhearted, Lisa confronted him. "I can't believe you've done this to me after I've tried so hard to please you! I've put up with all of your bullshit, I've made excuses for you, I've been patient, and you do this to me?"

To Lisa's astonishment, Tony denied everything. The more she insisted that he was having an affair, the angrier he got. They fought for hours. She kept at him, trying to get him to confess, but he adamantly denied it. She began to think that he was right and she was imagining the whole thing!

Of course, Lisa was right: Tony was having a casual affair with a young associate at work. When Lisa brought Tony along to her therapy session, he made it clear that he felt that Lisa's constant bitching at him justified his behavior. "She's always on my case. Always on me about stuff. I'm sorry for what I've done, but it was almost like I had no choice."

Although he'd been unhappy in the relationship for a long while, he didn't want to press the relationship's self-destruct button by admitting the meaningless affair. Although he'd never say it, Tony depended on Lisa. He secretly relied on her emotional support and consistency, despite her irritating, constant need to be around him all the time. The clandestine affair gave him a bit of breathing room from her suffocating need to always be with him. He found himself in a bind. He believed that if he admitted his indiscretion, her grip on him would only tighten that much more. She'd never give him a moment's peace. So he fought back, using his anger, cunning, and charm to deflect her incessant questions and keep her at arm's length.

Tony was using his affair as a way to put space between himself and Lisa. It was his "back door exit," through which he could escape when Lisa's demands for intimacy and affection became too shrill and unremitting. The more she pulled on his string, the more distance he placed between the two of them by retreating deeper and deeper into the affair. From his point of view, being frightened of getting close, he simply adapted to what he perceived as a threat to his independence and his sense of self.

Instead of communicating with Lisa that he wasn't getting his needs met in the relationship, Tony chose the easier alternative and sought to satisfy his needs with a new woman. The affair also gave him the illusion of separateness from Lisa, the feeling that he could escape to a safe distance when things got too close and uncomfortable with her. Telling lies to Lisa gave him a sense of autonomy and superiority. By keeping his affair a secret, he shut her out and created a barrier between them, a barrier that he felt was also a lifeline. It enabled him to retreat into his cave, distance himself from the uncomfortable issues that Lisa—in her equally ineffective way—kept demanding that he confront.

When the truth finally came out, Tony quickly adopted a strategy of self-justification. Like many men who are confronted with having an affair, Tony blamed Lisa for being too domineering, overbearing, and just plain "in my face about everything." Lisa wouldn't define herself in the same way but agreed with Tony that she was quite a strong woman. As with most couples I see in therapy who are dealing with these issues, the men see their partners as being in a position of power. Like the men on *Tool Academy*, Tony felt that Lisa had an endgame. In his mind, she was always trying to steer the relationship in the direction of marriage. Tony would say, "I am a man, no one tells me what to do. I am too young to settle down." But, of course, he is not single and playing the field; he is in a relationship and draws much of his strength from Lisa in the same way that a child would from a parent.

Whenever Tony misbehaved by getting drunk and forgetting to meet her at a restaurant or some other agreed-upon place, Lisa got mad, told him off, forgave him, and then expected better behavior from him the next time—just like a good mom. Or when he stayed out late getting plastered, she scolded him when he came through the door and then gave him a hug of forgiveness. Lisa created a safe and nurturing environment for Tony to go out and explore the world . . . all at her expense. Similar to the relationship he had when he was growing up, Tony was extracting from Lisa the support, intimacy, and understanding he had received from his mother when he was a child. Think back to session 6, where you listed all of the traits that you have taken from your guy's emotional bucket, enabling him to play the opposite role. Similarly, Lisa was being responsible, accountable, and levelheaded so that Tony could be irresponsible and unaccountable and act crazy.

Tony regarded Lisa as a powerful partner, and, like many men who seek refuge in an affair, he sought to redefine the power equation in the relationship by keeping a secret from Lisa. He had one over on her. It was his way of taking back some of the power he felt was all in Lisa's control. Lisa would eventually realize that Tony's cheating was an expression of his being underpowered, his attempt to take back some of the power he could not achieve through more direct means. As we worked together in therapy, Lisa understood that Tony simply didn't have the skills to adjust the balance in the relationship in an open and clear way.

Affairs are a symptom, not the cause, of a relationship in trouble. Affairs usually occur when all else has failed, as a last desperate attempt to rectify the unhappiness that results from a constricting relationship. It is lamentable that it takes the bombshell of betrayal for a couple to confront the suffering they are both enduring. Often, though, if the woman is honest, she'll confess that she buried her suspicions long before the final piece of evidence makes the affair impossible to ignore any longer.

The women on *Tool Academy* knew their men were cheating—maybe not in a concrete or factual way, but they knew it, nonetheless. They sensed immediately that something was wrong. Yet even though their guys were lousy liars, the women couldn't bring themselves to face the possibility that their men had cheated or were cheating on them. Women know instinctively when they are being lied to, however, and those lies chip away at and erode the relationship. Trust between them begins to crumble. The relationship is in peril.

The woman expends a tremendous amount of psychic energy denying the reality that her man is having an affair. She is practically driven crazy by her unconscious suspicion and is consumed by the need for constant reassurance of his affection and love. It's the classic Pursuer and Distancer dance.

Trust is the most precious and fragile commodity a relationship can create between two people. Once the slightest grain of deception is introduced, attempts at communication and reconciliation result in failure. The couple cannot achieve intimacy or grow, and the relationship suffers paralysis.

It Just Doesn't Add Up

Cheating is an unsustainable situation for both parties. The one who is having the affair has it no better off, however. Tony's affair may have eased one kind of tension in the relationship, but it also created its own special type of strain and pressure. He had to handle the desire, excitement, and pleasure, as well as the uncertainty, defensiveness, and anxiety, all outside of the relationship he had with Lisa. I often hear men say, "It's just sex," as a way to convey that they are able to compartmentalize the affair and separate it from their primary relationship. Yet what happens is that the guilt and anxiety generated by the affair have to be squelched, and soon the man's negative emotions overflow and are directed at his partner. For no good reason, he'll act moody or irritable or fly into a rage. Things he might have normally taken in stride will bother him. Making simple domestic decisions will confuse him. Finances might suddenly become an issue.

These are the symptoms of emotional excess, which adversely affect your relationship and give you the clues that he is being unfaithful. You can sense that your partner's strange behavior does not originate from the daily routine of your lives. At some level, you are aware that it just doesn't make sense, doesn't add up. This disconnect between what you know about your man and your relationship and the way he's now acting causes you to feel confused, frightened, defensive, and insecure.

You might want to try this three-part exercise to support your intuition and check whether he is cheating.

EXERCISE

Is He Cheating?

1. Use the String Theory. Test whether he reacts with unusual and unexplained behavior when you pull extra hard on his string. For example, make especially rigorous demands on him this week, and see whether he phones you up at four

o'clock in the afternoon to say he'll be working late and then comes home at an hour when he knows you'll be in bed, probably asleep.

2. Is he displaying unusual behavior? When you have agreed to a Saturday night dinner party at your sister's home, does he disappear for twenty, thirty minutes at a time, and when you ask where he's been, can he only come up with a lame excuse, like out smoking a cigarette or handling a problem at work on the phone?

3. Examine your lens sentence. Because it is likely that your lens sentence and his will be similar, think about how your lens sentence can make you feel and imagine how he would react to those same feelings. If your sentence is "I feel I am not good enough," then what would he be doing right now to alleviate the pain of feeling "not good enough?"

○ ○ ○

Your partner is sending you plenty of unconscious communication. Remember, he's conflicted about what he's up to. In his unconscious desire to be found out, he's dropping all kinds of hints and clues. The secret he's keeping from you takes its toll every time he lies or acts deviously. Listen to your intuition. You can sense when he's straying from his normal routine or behavior.

When the infidelity is finally revealed, both members of the couple are actually somewhat relieved. When Lisa finally found out about Tony's affair, she realized that she was not going crazy. All of his bizarre and disjointed behavior suddenly made sense. Yet her realization of Tony's affair also had the effect of rewriting their roles—and not necessarily in a productive way. The power in the relationship shifted again, but this time into Lisa's terrain. Yes, she felt hurt and humiliated, but she also began to experience the power that came from defining herself as a "victim," "the injured party." To put it simply, she felt that she was "in the right" and that Tony was "in the wrong." And until Lisa found a way to constructively reconcile the balance in the relationship and open channels of safe and productive communication, the knowledge that Tony was having an affair, which was now out in the open, only served to make Tony feel more underpowered. These were the dynamics that led Tony to cheat in the first place!

After he confessed to having an affair, Lisa thought long and hard about whether she wanted to stay with him and work things out. Eventually, she decided that she did. If you are faced with the discovery that your man has cheated, however, you may decide differently.

Do You Stay or Do You Go?

Your position in the relationship was compromised before your man confessed to his unfaithfulness. His secret kept the relationship off balance, and the power always tilted in his direction. But now you know, and the equality in the relationship has been restored. Maybe the power has even tipped your way. You can choose to leave or to stay. Naturally, there will be many other factors to consider. Can you financially afford to split up? Where will you live if you are the one who has to physically move out of your home? If you have children, how will they be cared for and looked after? These are all momentous considerations, but at least you are no longer living in fear of losing your mind.

Once trust has been violated, I often think the relationship resembles a broken vase: with patience and understanding as the glue, the pieces can be put back together again. If you look carefully, the cracks will always show, and the vase's shape will be forever altered. It's up to you. You decide. The relationship can be reconstructed, if you want it to be. The intimacy and trust can be rebuilt, if you are willing to work at this and if you decide you want to invest the time and emotion that are necessary to give it another try. The only way you will be successful is to peel back the layers and get to the real reason the affair occurred in the first place. Are you willing to hear and understand

why he cheated? Are you prepared to provide him with the missing
pieces of the relationship that he went looking for in seeking an affair
with another woman? Is he willing to do the work that's necessary to
regain your trust, and can he communicate what he felt was missing?
If you said yes, and you know he is saying yes, too, now is the time to
get out your tool kit and get down to business.

• •

Open Your Notebook

Like Tony's, your partner's probable first reaction will be—
incredibly!—to blame you. Imagine him listing the reasons
he cheated. Write them down in your notebook. Here is a list
I've put together from listening to women over the years, to
help you get started.

- You suffocate me.
- You don't listen to me.
- I can't talk to you.
- You pick fights with me.
- You don't support me.
- You are not good in bed.
- You're cheating on me.
- You think you own me.
- You want to tie me down.
- You get all of my attention, and nothing is ever enough.
- You don't really care what I do with my time.
- You're boring.
- You crowd me, and I need more space.
- You mean more to me than she does.
- You don't really love me, and I don't love you.

• •

EXERCISE

Listen to the Truth

Now it's time to have a conversation with your guy. In this exercise, I want you to find out the real reason that he thinks he's had the affair. If you are going to be able to coax him into a safe zone where he will feel okay about telling you why he cheated, you will need to use all of your active listening skills acquired from session 1. Don't expect the conversation to be pleasant or even civil. It will spark pain and anger, rebuke and recrimination. So before it escalates into a full-blown argument, remember your distancing techniques from session 5 and use them. Keep yourself in the position of an observer and give him some safe space, just as you learned in session 4. It is important that you stay calm during these initial conversations. You'll need to encourage him to tell you all of the facts so that you know exactly what you are dealing with and how to respond. I also recommend that you don't have this conversation more than a couple of times, only enough times to clearly understand and hear his reasons.

These initial conversations are critical, not only because they will give you the information you need to take back control of the situation but also because you are setting a conversational tone that will be productive and help you steer the relationship in the direction you want to take it. The more you know about the "why" of the affair, the better position you'll be in to take charge of your future relationship with him.

Here are some pointers that will help you have these discussions on your terms and stay in control.

Maintain eye contact with your partner. At this early juncture, it may be painful to look at him. Just as likely, his shame may also make it hard for him to look you in the eye. But eye contact is one of the most primal forms of communication. What you are feeling is communicated directly to your partner, bypassing the language center of the brain, where your emotions get translated into words that can often be clumsy and get misinterpreted, especially at times of stress like these.

Let your partner have his say. You will probably be upset and very emotional at first and will have the urge to scream at him or run out of the room. These are natural and appropriate responses. But try to listen to what he is saying without interrupting him or shouting him down. You need to hear the full story in order to assess exactly what happened and how you are going to handle it. What he says and how he says it will give you invaluable clues to help you decode the affair and gain insights into why it happened.

Keep your questions on the "why" of the affair. At this point, resist your need to know all of the details of the affair. You will want to know when and where he hooked up with her, was she a better lover, who made the first pass, how often they saw each other, and how often they had sex? But right now, control the conversation and focus on why he feels the affair happened. For example, ask your partner what he felt was going on in your relationship that necessitated his having an affair. What did the affair provide him with? What did he feel that he needed?

Avoid blaming him. Avoid blaming his lover. It will be tempting to cast your partner as a louse, a worthless, uncaring Tool! You will also have some choice words for the woman he betrayed you with: whore, bitch, home-wrecker, tramp. But as much as you will want to hurl insults at them and it may make you feel better temporarily, it will not genuinely help you work out why the affair happened.

Don't blame yourself! You may doubt your femininity and sexuality. You may tell yourself that you were the cause of why he ran into the arms of another woman. I'm here to tell you to stop. In the final analysis, affairs are shared responsibilities; you have joint custody for what happened. It's as erroneous to think the affair was entirely your fault as it is mistaken to believe that his infidelity was entirely his.

At first, like Tony, your man might go on the offensive, shouting and acting up, creating a smoke screen to hide his true feelings from both you and himself. This is simply to distract you, wear you down. He's depriving you of your well-deserved indignation and protecting himself from feeling bad. He might act all puffed up and tough, almost proud of his infidelity and his ability to put you in your place. But stick to the techniques you've learned. You may be a bit in shock, which will make you numb to the emotions you think you ought to be feeling. If you begin to argue, remember to disengage before you reach your flash point. Control the conversation, and make him meet you in a space where you both can communicate rationally and intelligently, even if it causes you some pain. And listen very, very carefully, because what you'll begin to hear will probably surprise you.

As you manage the conversation and adjust the emotional barometer, you'll begin to pick up verbal fragments that tell you that your guy feels inadequate and anxious. He'll begin to say things that betray his deep inner feelings of uncertainty, jealousy, and low self-esteem. But hold on! Aren't these the emotions that he is making *you* feel, while he's been running around acting like Mr. Stud? You'll recognize what's really going on if you recall the lessons of session 6. He's taken the feelings that make him feel uncomfortable and has poured them into your emotional buckets. But now that his secret is out in the open, with the cause for all of your insecure and jealous feelings exposed, you can stop feeling those terribly disempowering emotions.

Before you can let go of the negative feelings he has imposed on you, he'll need to be crystal clear that his cheating is over. It is imperative he tells you openly that he has stopped or will stop the cheating. And he has to say it with conviction. He's got to mean it, and he's got to make you believe him. Only then will he be able to absorb some of the bad feelings you are now going to share with him and only then will it release you to feel some of the anger you're entitled to. Remember, he is unaccustomed to, and frightened of, feeling the emotions that are about to be put back into his buckets.

So go slowly at every challenge you encounter in this session. It will take a little time for him to get used to feeling like an adult.

EXERCISE

It's Your Turn to Rant

I know you've been very patient up until now. You've listened to your partner without reprisal or recrimination while he fluctuated between bragging about his affair and being all tearful, wimpy, and repentant. You've heard what he's had to say, and now it is your turn. In this next phase, I want you to give full expression to your pent-up feelings of hurt, anger, and disappointment. Your emotions are beginning to kick in, and you need to get them out into the open. Say whatever you need to say to him. Call him names. Curse him. Scream at him for how he's taken advantage of you.

Now's the time to let it all out. Get out of him whatever you need to know. If it's all of the gory details of the affair, well, then make him tell you. But here's the catch. You are to have this session only twice a week and only for thirty-minute intervals. During those two half-hour sessions, you can really go at it. Break dishes, shout at the top of your lungs, tell him exactly what you think of him—but only during the allotted time. For the rest of the week, you need to hold off and subdue your angry, bitter, hurt feelings, until it's time to vent them according to the prearranged schedule.

That's the deal, and he's got to abide by it as well. If he's not willing to enter into the agreement, then he needs to be reminded that you are the victim, that he was the one who betrayed the trust and screwed around, while you waited for him at home. The least he can do is appease you in this one instance. I am quite sure, as I have found with so many of my clients, that he'll be grateful that he's going to be the punching bag for only sixty minutes a week, and he'll think he's getting off easy.

Limiting the expression of the hurt and pain that you feel and the shame and guilt he feels will allow the relationship to heal. The two of you have been through a terrible ordeal. It's a whole new ball game now, and both of you need time to try it on for size, to see how it feels. He is vulnerable now that his secret is out in the open, and he has your attention. You are no longer haunted by suspicions now that you know about his indiscretion. You don't always need to be on the attack and nag him to be more intimate and affirm his love for you. Many couples report to me that they feel closer to each other during at this phase than they have in ages.

Rebuild the Trust

The next step in retooling your relationship is to rebuild the shattered trust. In many ways, you are a different person now than you were when you began this book. The skills you have acquired and the exercises you practiced have changed your perspective on your relationship (and revealed different facets of yourself, too). You might realize now that blind trust is an adolescent attribute, because in an adult relationship complete trust is always at risk.

• •

Open Your Notebook

Now is a perfect time to think about trust and how it is created in the relationship. In your notebook, make a list of the qualities that you think are essential if trust is to be reborn in your relationship. Here are some of the elements that are important to many people. They may be useful to you, too, but feel free to add your own.

- Reliability
- Predictability

- Honesty
- Loyalty
- Commitment
- Shared boundaries

• •

You are now ready to come full circle from the discussion you first had when you discovered your partner's cheating. You are going to do this by having another discussion in which, once again, you mainly listen. You'll need to probe, however. It's up to you to ask him questions that will connect what he is saying to many of the qualities you've outlined in your "trust" list.

When asking questions about his affair, be bold and fearless but also be honest and respectful. "If another woman came into your life whom you found attractive and were hot for, how would you act?" "If you were having drinks late one night with another woman, would you come home and tell me?" You are ready to listen deeply to what he has to say. The skills and the insights you now possess will help you better understand what you need to know to move forward. Trust your instincts. You will know whether you can believe his answers. You are much wiser than you were when you first had these conversations.

New Relationship Guidelines

It will take more than a change of heart on his part and yours if the relationship is going to move forward. For the relationship to really go to the next level, he will have to translate those good intentions into real behavior. In this next set of exercises, I'll ask you to make two lists that will help you control how he will give shape and form to his desire to be more of a man and less of a Tool.

• •

Open Your Notebook

Open your notebook and make a list of how your man needs to behave if he is to have a future with you. Here are some suggestions to use as a springboard for your own ideas.

- I want you to compliment me when I look nice or do a good job at work or around the house.

- I want you to be on time when we arrange to meet.

- I want you to be more tolerant of my family.

- I want you to initiate sex more regularly.

- I want you to go shopping with me occasionally.

- I want to feel as if I can go to you with my problems and that you won't bite my head off or make me feel stupid.

- I want you to encourage me to try new activities.

Now, review your list and read it through his eyes. After all, the exercises you practiced in this book have helped you develop your ability to identify and understand his feelings or difficulties. So use your empathy now and make another list of what you believe he requires for the relationship to go forward. He is your guy, you know him. Think about what he truly would like you to do more of, in order to feel that his needs are being met. Don't let the examples below limit you. Everyone is different. Your list will be right for your relationship.

- I want you to make me feel better when I have a bad day and not be made to feel that it's my fault.

- I want you to still find me attractive, even though I'm sometimes scared and in over my head at work.

- I want you to understand that I'm still friends with my ex and be confident that she's not a threat to you.

- I want you to get wild in bed.

- I want you to show a bit more appreciation when I take you out to dinner and spend money on you.

• •

Rebuilding Shattered Trust

Solidifying your relationship after the trauma of a betrayal will take time, and you need to be patient. There will be setbacks and break-throughs. It is important that you hold your ground, or the lessons you've given him will be short-lived and forgotten. Both of you have a lot of growing to do. And because you have the insight and awareness of what is really going on inside the relationship, you are in charge. You are giving him what he needs to feel more secure, confident, and giving. You control the boundaries of the partner-ship so that his emotional needs are satisfied within the context of the relationship you provide to him.

Will he be true to you forever and ever? Will you be true to him forever and ever? No one can say. Life is uncertain. But you now have a yardstick to measure how the relationship is going, and you will feel the warning signs if the relationship goes off the rails before it tumbles over the cliff.

For many readers, this will have been one of the most painful ses-sions of the book. For some, the exercises and insights in this session have helped make it possible to regain the trust that was shattered when their partners cheated. These readers should select the seventh gift on their list of rewards. Think of it as a Trust badge.

For others, the wounds are still too raw. These women have also found the inner strength to confront difficult truths and are willing to accept the underlying causes for their partners' infidelity, but their partners' acts of infidelity are too fresh for them to bestow their trust and give the relationship a second chance. The time may come when they will be ready to hand over their trust to their partners and attempt a fresh beginning. But in the meantime, for these women—perhaps you?—that moment is still far off. Regardless, you, too, have earned the right to a gift of self-congratulation and should grant yourself the indulgence listed in the seventh position on your list.

The undeniable fact is that you are stronger and more independent now; you have honed your instincts. If he does cheat on you again, you will recognize the signs and act on them accordingly. You have gained insight into yourself and know what your needs are better than before. You are the adult in the room and have the emotional resources to get what you want. If you can't get it with the man you're with now, then you are strong enough and courageous enough to look elsewhere.

Sex: The Ultimate Power Tool

What do you think about when you think about sex?

Sex is fun? Sex is a chore? Sex is exciting? Sex is naughty?

Sex is intimacy, a form of self-expression, a way to connect, or just plain necessary?

It can be, and often is, all of these things and much, much more. But if you are reading this book because you want to get control of your man and take charge of the relationship to obtain what you most desire, I want you to equate sex with power. Because it's the power you naturally possess over your partner.

Chances are, you are probably already savvy to the fact that if you want to take control of your relationship, you'll have to take control of the sex. And now you're ready to let me help you take it to the next level.

I hope that you understand and will agree that control is not necessarily a negative in a relationship. Actually, it is essential, as long as you are flexible and willing to relinquish it from time to time. But now,

I am encouraging you to take hold of the power that is your natural birthright and exert it to achieve what you want in your relationship.

His Power Tool: Money

Traditionally, in relationships, men hold power by controlling the finances. For a man, money is an expression of power, an extension of his masculine identity. When a couple fights about money, what the two people don't realize is that they are actually fighting about power and control. By controlling the acquisition of material possessions—the clothes you wear, the car you drive, the food you eat—the man controls much of what is necessary and enjoyable about your existence. So when you fight about whether you can buy that extra pair of shoes, it's as much about his controlling you and your pleasure as it is about whether he can afford it or you need another pair.

Most women I've helped in therapy readily acknowledge that men equate money with power. It's easy enough to understand in the abstract. But rarely do women fully comprehend how much that equation controls their everyday lives.

• •

Open Your Notebook

To demonstrate the extent that women often relinquish the control of money, and therefore some portion of power in their relationships, answer the following questions in your notebook and see just how much power your guy holds by controlling the purse strings.

> How much can you spend without checking with your guy? $10, $50, $100, $500, $1,000, or more?
>
> How much can he spend without checking with you? $10, $50, $100, $500, $1,000, or more?
>
> Are the finances divided into *his* money and *your* money, or do you pool everything?

Who makes the major decisions about when and how to spend money on household items? On vacations? Cars?

Who earns the most money?

Do you know how much he earns?

Does he know how much you spend on clothes?

Do you know how much he spends on clothes?

Do you know how much money he spends supporting other members of his family? Would you ask him to do the same for your family?

Does he let you see his checkbook and/or his credit card statements?

• •

Open Your Notebook

Assign a value reflecting the financial importance (low, medium, high) to the following items for you and for your partner.

Item	*You*	*Him*
Car		
Entertainment		
Clothes		
House		
Books/magazines/videos/CDs		
Computers/TVs/DVDs		
Vacations		
Restaurants/bars/clubs		
Gym memberships		
Charitable giving		
Paying the household bills		

Mortgage/rent

Health insurance and arranging
    doctor visits

Remembering special occasions
    and buying gifts

• •

It's not unusual for couples to keep their finances a secret from each other, never discussing the subject. I've had women in my therapy office who'd been married for twenty-odd years and had no idea how much money their husbands earned!

Money is one of the main topics that couples fight about, but it is only the battleground, not the battle. Issues involving money pervade a relationship and are the man's main source of leverage when it comes to control. That's why when a woman makes more money than her husband or boyfriend, roles can get confused, and the man usually has to find other ways to define his masculinity and exert himself in the relationship.

Sex Is Your Currency

To even the odds, women quite logically and naturally use sex to exert their influence in a relationship. Sex is our currency, and we need to spend or save it wisely and purposefully if we are going to acquire the desired value and quality from our relationships with our men.

Throughout this session, we'll work with the notion that sex—more intimate and satisfying sex—is really the by-product of a core concept I've discussed in regard to other areas of your relationship: namely, better communication. You've seen an example of this in the previous session when we explored the reasons a man might cheat on his partner. For many men, better sex may be the reason that he thinks he's running into the arms of another women, but the real reason, as you've discovered, is to balance the power scale in the relationship. When a woman is perceived as being too powerful and therefore too threatening or too domineering or too maternal, the man seeks to remedy the power equation by having sex with another woman. Sex is not really the problem.

Typically, the struggle for power that occurs in the sexual arena emerges once the romantic love stage of the relationship has ended. Women are absolutely convinced that their men deliberately withhold the intimacy and affection that they feel have left the relationship. When women find themselves in this predicament, they often exhibit the classic stages of grief; the sense of loss, of being deprived of the illusion of romantic love, is every bit as real and painful as the physical loss of a loved one.

First, you feel shock. The emotional landscape has suddenly changed, and what was once familiar and comfortable is now strange and foreign. You find yourself wondering, Can this man who is lying next to me in bed be the person I am going to spend the rest of my life with? Next, you try to rationalize the scary situation you find yourself in by interpreting your man's shortcomings and faults in a positive way. You think, Maybe he's having a tough time at work. Maybe his family is giving him grief. Maybe it's something about me that he has suddenly discovered to be unattractive or repellent.

What follows is a phase of anger: After all, who does he think he is? I've put up with all of his little quirks and nonsense. I've made sacrifices. So where does he get off acting so aloof, able to make time and be available for everyone but me? Yet even though many women find themselves furious with their men at this stage, they are not willing or able to confront their partners with their dissatisfaction or break off the relationships altogether. So, in desperation, as we have seen, many women make the mistake of taking an aggressive and antagonistic approach to change their partners' behavior. They nag, criticize, badger, and hassle their men in the hope of changing them. This is the bargaining phase of grief, in which women, in order to achieve some small amount of satisfaction, start to make compromises.

There's that word again: compromise. You know from session 4 that one of the biggest differences between my approach to helping women in their relationships and the advice of many other therapists is that I don't believe couples entering therapy should make any more compromises to achieve emotional balance and harmony in their relationships. Women make so many compromises in their lives already, and there is nothing to be gained by also compromising their satisfaction with their relationships. Furthermore, compromise in a relationship simply doesn't work. Sooner or later, the unhappiness, reproach, and frustration creep back in, further deepening and prolonging the grief cycle. And that's when despair sets in, the last stage of the power struggle.

So many of the women I've worked with who have gone down this path are unable to break the cycle and call it quits, ending the relationship with separation or divorce. My guess is that if you are reading this book, you are somewhere in the middle phases of the grief cycle, and you have a good chance of creating a positive and rewarding outcome for yourself.

BREAK THE SEXUAL STALEMATE

The first step is to take control and break the sexual stalemate. It's an all-too-familiar standoff: you need intimacy for sex, and he needs sex for intimacy. In a sense, each of you wants the same thing, but because you are a woman and he is a man, each of you goes about getting it in ways that are ingrained in the psyche of your gender. You need more involvement, verbal reassurance, and tangible contact prior to having sex, while he needs sex before he can let down his guard and demonstrate his tender side.

GIVE AND YOU'LL GET

There are other important differences between how men and women function psychologically, as well as biologically, that need to be addressed, and I'll discuss them shortly. But right now, I want you to be aware that he probably wants to feel close and intimate (just as much as you do!), but his way of achieving it is through the physical act of sex. Although you may believe that withholding sex is a way to exert your power, by withholding sex you are actually working against yourself. By misapplying your sexual power in this way, you are in reality denying him the only pathway he has available to fulfill your needs for intimacy. This session will show you how to use your sexual power to achieve the intimacy you want by controlling your sexual currency. And, yes, you will be training him as well so that he gives you the pleasure you've been missing.

IT'S ALL ABOUT CHEMISTRY

In order to have great sex, you'll need a basic understanding of how men and women experience sex differently. Gender plays a huge role in the biology, as well as in the psychology, of sex. Research tells us that men generally have a higher sex drive. It's a bit more complicated than the idea that men are simply horny all the time and will take any and every opportunity to get off. Testosterone is the hormone that's largely responsible for a person's sex drive, and typically, a man has twenty to forty times more of it coursing through his body than an average woman does. A woman's testosterone level (and other sex-enhancing hormones and hence her sex drive) fluctuates on a monthly basis, being dramatically affected by her monthly period, as well as by having children. A man's testosterone level, on the other hand, stays pretty much the same throughout his early adult life.

Another difference between the sexes is the way a man and a woman express their sex drive. Typically, men tend to behave more assertively than women when it comes to sex. Women are much more complex. Their sex drive is influenced not only by testosterone but also by the female hormone estrogen. Unlike the "assertive" inclinations generated by testosterone, estrogen is more "receptive." There is a huge distinction between being passive and being receptive. High levels of estrogen enable women to be more approachable, open, friendly, sympathetic, and seductive—qualities that translate quite nicely and naturally into the bedroom. For men, sex can be just sex, while a woman may also want to use sex as a way to express intimacy or to please her partner.

In the early days of a relationship, both men and women tend to have much higher sex drives. Evolutionary psychologists suggest that this is important because nature dictates that one of our most primal instincts is the need to reproduce, so that the species has the best possible chance of survival. It's called "pair bonding," but over time the sex drive falls off—particularly for women. The result is that both men and women find themselves confused. Men feel betrayed and rejected by their former "sex-kitten" partners and are afraid that their partners' declining desire for sex means that there is a problem in the relationship. Women wonder whether their diminishing sex drive means that they don't love their partners as much as they used to. Yet in reality, these changes in desire are simply the natural course of events in any couple's relationship.

The Sex Cycle

If you are having problems with sex or are not having much of it, it is nearly impossible to jump-start the process by hopping into bed and being a willing partner. So, let's start by reviewing the sex cycle that I introduced in session 1.

As you would expect, a woman's sex cycle operates differently from a man's, given the differences in their biological chemistry. Both sexes share the sex cycle's five stages: desire, arousal, plateau, orgasm, and resolution (see the following illustration). But for women, the

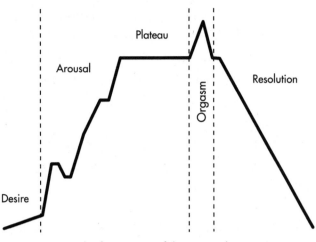

The five stages of the sex cycle.

phases of the cycle vary much more dramatically in duration and intensity. And your individual five-phase cycle is unique to you and you alone. Each of these phases needs to be completed before you move onto the next, for you to have satisfying sex.

ARE YOU IN THE MOOD?

It all begins with desire. Desire is one of the most important aspects of successful lovemaking because it gets things moving. Without desire, sex can be unpleasant or may simply not happen at all. In the beginning of the relationship, romantic love triggers the necessary chemistry for desire, so that sex is plentiful and pleasurable. But once the illusion of romantic love wears off and other emotions begin to surface, desire can fade or be increasingly intermittent, with the collateral damage being the diminishing quality of your lovemaking.

Men can jump the desire phase altogether and become physically aroused and primed for the plateau period very quickly. They have a very obvious anatomical barometer right in front of them to signal whether they are ready for sex. They are more easily aroused by visual stimuli (the sight of your body), as well as by sounds, smells, and even memories.

Most women, however, require a more prolonged state of desire for successful sex. But true desire is a fragile commodity. Resentment, fatigue, stress—there are many internal feelings and external circumstances that can have a harmful effect on your sex cycle so that the fuse of desire never gets lit. You need to feel warm, relaxed, playful, a bit vulnerable, trusting, and sensitive—all of the things that you may feel have vanished in the current state of your relationship. So it's no wonder that sex has been a problem.

It's a vicious cycle. If you could manage to have sex more regularly, then feelings of intimacy would be more accessible, because your boyfriend is getting what he needs to be intimate with you. But I'm guessing you don't feel close enough with your partner right now to want to start your cycle. If the cycle breaks down, it becomes increasingly more difficult to kick-start it again. For example, after a few sessions in which your arousal stage is not achieved, when the next opportunity for sex presents itself, you are less likely to be inclined to start the process. Sex becomes a "no go" zone for couples who let the situation languish. You will want to avoid sex because you know where it is heading: frustration at not getting sufficiently aroused, feeling that your needs are being ignored, being left behind as the man rushes on to the next part, and maybe difficulty reaching an orgasm.

AROUSAL EQUALS EXCITEMENT

Desire is mostly mental. It puts you in the mood. The next stage is arousal, and it has more of a physical element to it. Arousal is usually associated with foreplay and needs to be of sufficient duration to prepare a woman for penetration. This is a precarious stage and is often left uncompleted. Arousal gets a woman ready for the physical act of lovemaking by allowing the man to enter the woman easily. As we have seen, a man's arousal cycle can be much more abbreviated than a woman's, which is why many men rush this phase of their partners' sex cycle. Kissing is very important for women to become aroused, and couples often neglect this component when they have been together for a long time.

We'll revisit the arousal stage a bit later in this session. I will show you how you can train your man to slow it down, lengthening this phase so that you can be better prepared, both physically and mentally, for sex.

GETTING IT ON

The plateau phase is the heightened level of excitement when you lose yourself in your partner and in your lovemaking. When women reach the plateau stage, they can stay there for quite some time before having an orgasm. Too often, though, the plateau phase is rushed. Again, sex can become just a means "to get off," rather than a couple enjoying a heightened sense of connection. When men start the run-up to their orgasm, once the orgasm mechanism has engaged, it creates a momentum all of its own, and ejaculation has to follow. Men actually cannot stop their orgasm. It takes time, skill, and communication to sync up your sex cycle with your guy's.

ORGASM

A woman can easily be put off if the arousal period is rushed or her man has an orgasm too early. She may not be well lubricated or may not be sufficiently excited, while he is off and running without her, which leaves her feeling left behind. Sadly, I have found that women often blame themselves for what they perceive to be their poor sexual performance. They believe it is their fault that they take too long to become aroused, that their needs are not as important or as urgent as their men's. Research tells us that only a small percentage of women have orgasms from penetration alone, so it does no good that he is banging away if you have not been prepared by foreplay: kissing, touching, stroking, oral sex, or masturbation.

Many women would rather fake orgasms than discuss their sex cycles with their partners, but remember, good sex is all about communication. Men usually have trouble when it comes to talking about their techniques in bed. Don't assume your partner can read your mind about what you need to help you have an orgasm. It is very important to be able to talk about what you want and what you like. The best time to talk about sex is when you are not having it. Try to discuss sex specifically when you are not in the bedroom— for example, maybe when you are out taking a walk or having a meal together.

The next part of the sex cycle is the physical act of making love, when you are aroused, highly sensitized, and ready to orgasm. During lovemaking, the best way to get more of what you like is to let him know what you enjoy. When he touches you the right way, encourage him by letting out a soft moan, move his body or hand to direct him, while showing that he is pleasuring you. If you like something he does, then make sure you let him know. Believe me, he'll notice if your communication is clear and definite. You are in charge. You will be training your man by giving him positive feedback when he makes love to you in a way you find pleasurable. If possible, it also helps if you physically perform a move on him that you'd like him to do to you. You need to teach him. Don't be shy about giving him ideas. Most men are truly eager to please and will comply with your gentle and tender instruction, if they think it will help them be better lovers.

RESOLUTION: INTIMACY IS YOUR SHARED REWARD

Once both partners are physically satisfied, they enter the fifth and final phase of lovemaking. Many women report to me that most of their problems arise during this resolution phase. They feel that the intimacy created by their lovemaking is abruptly lost because their partners turn on the TV, roll over and fall asleep, or get up and wander off into the kitchen to fix themselves something to eat. My clients complain that all they are asking for is to curl up, cuddle, and talk. Instead of feeling close and connected to their lovers, they describe the phase following sex as the time when they feel most alone.

Sex is so emotionally charged and so much of the communication is nonverbal that it can be difficult to analyze and reach an understanding of what's stopping you from having satisfying sex. One of the biggest challenges is overcoming the urge to chuck it all in when you encounter an obstacle in your lovemaking. If you run into a glitch in your sex cycle, you naturally won't want to start again and risk another round of disappointment and feel that same acute sense of failure. So it is important that you fully understand your own personal sex cycle and are able to pinpoint the rough patches that can be smoothed out with the exercises presented in this session.

The Sex Wheel and the Sex Cycle Revisited

• •

Open Your Notebook

To help clarify the situation, I'd like you to open your notebook and redraw your sex wheel without consulting the one you created in session 1. Remember that the hub of the wheel is the physical act of sex, and the spokes coming out of the hub are the other categories in your life. Now compare the wheel you just drew with the one you created in session 1. Write down the differences that may have surfaced since you've been performing the exercises in this book.

Now do the same with the sex cycle (revisit your original answers to the sex cycle questions from session 1). Perhaps the actual arousal stage has improved because your communication skills have also been enhanced. It is also possible that the resolution phase has diminished lately, because you are still working out the best way to maneuver the relationship into the right balance between Pursuer and Distancer. You can see what is changing by comparing your two versions.

• •

• •

Open Your Notebook

Use your lens sentence to bring your sex cycle into sharper focus. Answer the following questions, and write down how they relate to your lens sentence.

- Are you lonely when the physical act of sex is consummated?

- Does sex feel hurried? Do you feel left behind, with your needs neglected, as you constantly try to catch up with the trajectory of his cycle?

- Is the sex activity always all about him?

- Does he demonstrate that he understands your physical requirements for sex?

- Is he attentive, responsive, and mindful of your needs, or do you need to reteach him what you like each time you have sex?

- If there is a problem with sex in the relationship, do you think it is your fault?

- Can you discuss sex freely and uninhibitedly?

- Does he always achieve orgasm first?

- During sex, do you feel shut out?

- Do you feel that he is totally absorbed in his pleasure?

- Do you feel that he is mechanically going through the motions of having sex?

- Does he respond when you perform new techniques in the bedroom?

• •

LEARNING FROM SARA AND MARK

When Sara, whom we met in session 4, answered these questions using her lens sentence ("I am never good enough"), she discovered that her sex cycle had several areas of vulnerability.

Sara, if you remember, was very needy. She repeatedly sought reassurance and expressions of affection from Mark, her partner. I saw it on a number of occasions when they were in therapy together. Mark would be talking, and Sara, feeling left out and neglected, blurted out questions about whether Mark had noticed that she was wearing a new top or a pair of shoes and whether he liked them. If he didn't respond right away, she recoiled, feeling belittled and demeaned. If she pressed him for an answer and he replied affirmatively but not convincingly, she would get upset and appeal to me, attempting to draw me into their skirmish. "You don't fool me and you don't fool Trina," she said, practically shouting at him. "She can see through you just as easily as I can."

At times like this, I saw that nothing he could say or do would remedy the situation. The more he tried to convey his sincere feelings toward her, the more she felt that he was trying to put one over on her. "You're such a lousy liar," she would say. "I can't believe a word you say." When he lost all hope in trying to appeal to her regarding his honest intentions, he turned to me, laying out a defense for himself like an accused convict and addressing me as if I were the judge, jury, and executioner. Nothing he did, however, seemed sufficient or genuine enough to satisfy Sara's underlying suspicion that she just didn't measure up.

Her feelings of inadequacy would intrude and short-circuit in varying degrees each of the five phases of her sex cycle. Initially, Sara's feelings of desire were undermined by her belief that she wasn't worthy of her partner's affections or that she was destined to fail at pleasing him. She had to work very hard at suppressing these feelings and overcoming her fears in order to even get to the beginning of her cycle: the desire phase. But the arousal phase was no easier for Sara, because here, too, she felt fearful and not very confident about her abilities to sexually stimulate her partner. She was plagued by doubts during their session of foreplay. Was she touching him the right way? Was that a moan of pleasure or disappointment she kept hearing? Was she exciting enough for him in bed? Her mind kept conjuring up all of his other girlfriends whom she knew about and how much more experienced they must have been. She knew Mark well enough to tell when he was approaching his orgasm, but again, her insecurity of not being a satisfying sex partner, of being so out of sync with him, meant that she was nowhere near ready for her orgasm.

Sara was never able to enjoy the intimacy of the third phase, the plateau, because she was always measuring herself against some unstated image of the perfect sex partner for her man, and she never got carried away. Needless to say, the resolution phase concluded equally unsatisfactorily for Sara. She never achieved orgasm, and in the aftermath of their lovemaking, no matter how Mark complimented her, Sara felt that he was just mouthing the words.

As it turned out, when Sara began to talk with Mark about their respective sexual needs, she learned that he was being perfectly sincere in his compliments about Sara's sex skills. What Sara learned from evaluating and viewing her sex cycle through her lens sentence was that she always experienced their lovemaking in terms of her partner's need, thus sabotaging her chances for satisfying sex. She totally neglected her own needs and subjugated her pleasure to her partner's. Sara soon realized that she could free herself from her feelings of inadequacy by simply accepting that she was good in bed with Mark and by being a bit more assertive about showing him how to satisfy her needs.

It never fails to surprise me that two people in a relationship assume they know what the other enjoys sexually and never bother to ask. Don't expect your man to know how you like to be touched or what you want to do in bed. Men aren't born perfect lovers. Your guy needs to be taught by you, because your needs are special and unique to you and you alone. And don't think that just because he has a penis, he knows what to do with it. Gently and tenderly, show him how you want him to use it. It is very rare that a man is not somewhat anxious about his performance and would rather avoid asking questions to find out. Women, on the other hand, face the challenging task of communicating with their men to get their needs met. The result is that men try harder at the wrong things, and women are not able to tell them what they are doing wrong.

Sex Is Off the Menu

It may be a bit counterintuitive, but the best way I know for a woman to get her man to jump-start her sex cycle is to abstain for a time from actually having sex with him. Let me be clear. I don't mean refraining from having physical contact with him. In the following exercise, I'll be encouraging you to touch him (and him, you!) in various exciting and exotic ways that are entirely sensual without being directly sexual.

EXERCISE

Sensual Touch

The act of intercourse is so powerful and emotionally charged that for purposes of this exercise, I tell couples that sex is off limits for now. That's because I want you to learn to generate and control the feeling of desire and intimacy between the two of you. To do that, you will need to experience each other slowly and closely. You'll have to learn how to give and take sensual pleasure, generating desire without expectation or pressure to perform intercourse. Here's how.

Tell him that you have a surprise for him, something very special that you want to give him. Play the actress and be coy, alluring, enticing. Let him believe that what he is about to receive will be all about him. Naturally, he'll think what he's about to get is sex. But what you will offer him is something much better suited for the situation. Because intercourse is such a high-stakes game at the moment, tell him that you are going to make him feel good for an evening, in any way he chooses, just as long as it doesn't involve sex. When he stops and thinks about it, that leaves the field of activity pretty wide open. You can bathe him, massage him, tickle him with a feather, whatever he wants, just as long as it doesn't involve touching an erogenous zone or actually having sex.

Most men have unsophisticated imaginations when it comes to this sort of thing. You'll need to have some activities already planned so that he gets the idea and will be able to come up with some of his own suggestions, too. Shampoo his hair. Rub oil on his feet and hands. Lick his stomach. The one thing he cannot do is touch you. If he wants to have sex, you must playfully insist that he wait for another time.

o o o

Remember: you are in charge. These are your rules, and you hold the power. If he tries to break the rules, then it's game over. What you'll accomplish is that while he thinks he's the Master and you're the Slave, in fact it's the other way round: you're the Master and he's the Slave. You're arousing his desire, exquisitely teasing him to be more sensual and sensitive to his body by example, slowing down the cycle, keeping it all at the desire phase. Again, I know this is all about giving him what *you* want, but you are setting the example so that he understands and experiences for himself the pleasure and intimacy you need. I am quite sure he will be eager to do the same to you in return.

When I give the Sensual Touch exercise as homework to couples who are having difficulty with sex, they are very responsive and eager to enter into the playfulness of the lesson. They actually seem relieved because sex is not allowed and the pressure is off. They can go back and reexperience a time like when they first met, reawakening the pleasure of giving and receiving sensual pleasure. Yet it is not uncommon for couples to come back the next week after being assigned this exercise and say, "Sorry, Trina, we started out the exercise just fine, but we got the homework all wrong and ended up having sex." Of course, they are rather pleased with themselves, and a breakthrough may have been achieved. So don't worry if the exercise takes an unexpected turn. But only after you have a few sessions of only nonsexual touching do I want you to give in and have intercourse. It's important that you first establish an appreciation for each other's physical selves, pure and simple.

Communicate Your Fantasies

In my practice, I have often observed that couples who are having trouble with their lovemaking find it easier to have sex than to talk about it. I have said and it's worth repeating: good sex is good communication. Sometimes, the situation calls for nonverbal communication, as when I asked you to touch your boyfriend in the way you want him to touch you. At other times, spoken words are required to get the job done.

EXERCISE

Let's Talk about Sex

This exercise is intended to help you overcome some of the uncomfortable and awkward feelings that couples often experience when they talk about their sex lives. It's an exciting and fun way to use conversation to put you in control of syncing up his sex cycle with yours, and it gets him to be attentive to the unfulfilled phases of your cycle. The exercise centers on each of you sharing your sexual fantasies.

I want you to select a moment when you are both involved in an activity, whether it be walking, relaxing, or making dinner together. Set the mood by turning on your inner flirt, and have some sweet fun with him in that special way that only you know how to do. You are probably still a bit angry with him, but remember: changing patterns of behavior is difficult and will feel a bit weird and forced at first. The reward for your efforts will be better communication in your sex life, yielding greater intimacy and enjoyment.

○ ○ ○

When he starts to respond to your overtures, maneuver the conversation to the topic of sexual fantasies. It's not as big a leap as you might think. Some simple phrases can serve as a comfortable and easy transition, such as, "You know, I was talking today with one of my girlfriends about her sexual fantasies . . ." or "I read in the paper the other day that loads of couples share their sexual fantasies with their partners . . ."

Then ask him what some of his sexual fantasies are. You may want to phrase it a little less directly, such as, "What would you like to do sexually that we haven't done?" or "What is your favorite sexual fantasy?" This may pleasantly surprise him, embarrass him, or even shock him a bit. But use your feminine magic and get him to open up.

Many people have very active and healthy fantasy lives, but they labor under the common misunderstanding that they need to act out their fantasies, make them real. The usefulness of fantasies is often just that: to keep them imaginary, a tool to balance or offset their counterparts in reality. Some fantasies are never meant to be realized. Many people have secret, private fantasies that they use to kick off the desire phase of their sex cycles. Fantasies are a useful tool, but they do not need to be performed or even shared. A fantasy serves its purpose quite adequately by being yours and yours alone. It may be a mental image or a scenario, something make-believe that detaches you from everyday reality and helps you get aroused.

Remember that the purpose of this conversation is also about getting him to behave in bed in ways that will make you feel more fulfilled. So, fix in your mind the phase of your cycle that you want to be deeper, more slowed down, caressingly developed. Now that he's in the mood, it's time for you to play the kittenish detective and maneuver the conversation to entice him to tell you what he thinks really turns you on. Don't judge or shame him. Let him know subtly whether he's on target or not. If he is right, your response—a sly smile or a wink or a giggle perhaps—will guarantee that he'll repeat the desired behavior the next time you have sex. If he is mistaken and is reading you incorrectly, I suggest that you reply by agreeing with him but then follow up by suggesting another activity he could perform on you that would really rock your world. Guide him to the parts of your sex curve with coy verbal hints, and let him know where you want him to linger, to be more attentive or thoughtful.

Remember Lela and Sean from session 7? Lela, you'll recall, was the introvert, always shy and demure, never wanting to call attention to herself. Sean was the extrovert, the life of the party, the one who always loved to take on new challenges and was highly competitive at work and with his friends. When I began to broach the topic of their sex life, it was only too obvious that their self-assigned roles were also being played out there. Sean took command, initiating sex and controlling the pace of each phase of their lovemaking according to the timetable of his sex cycle. Lela followed his lead, utterly responsive and receptive to Sean's physical desires and needs. She thought herself to be the perfect partner for Sean because she knew what he liked and let him call all the shots in bed. At least, that was what she thought.

When Lela used her feminine wiles to get him to talk about their sex life, she was utterly shocked when he said that he would like it if she took more of an active role in their lovemaking. He said he found it a bit burdensome that it was always up to him to initiate sex, and it made him feel as if he was forcing it on her.

Then came the part of the conversation that really stunned her. When she suggested that he tell her a fantasy, he got red in the face and extremely shy. She gently coaxed it out of him, and she could hardly believe what he was saying. He wanted her not only to initiate sex, but it was his fantasy to have sex with his hands and feet tied to the bedposts! Sean's admission was quite revealing, because Lela understood how both members of a couple fill each other's emotional buckets with uncomfortable behaviors. Sean's fantasy of being submissive in bed meant that he was also secretly desirous of being less domineering on occasion.

As we know from meeting Lela previously, she wanted to take back some of the extroverted behaviors that she'd off-loaded and filled Sean's emotional buckets with. So Sean's admission of wanting her to be more aggressive in bed came as an incredibly happy surprise to her. It was her fantasy come true!

Lela took the next big step by connecting her lovemaking difficulties with the fears and insecurities expressed by her lens sentence. She was able to relate her abhorrence for standing out and drawing attention to herself to her introverted and passive behavior in the bedroom. If you feel ready, take out your lens sentence now and try to connect it with what you have discovered are the sticky points in your sex cycle.

Lela and Sean's relationship had turned a corner, to be sure. But it was still fragile, and sex was very much a tender issue. So I suggested that they carry out this next exercise, which follows quite naturally from the previous exercise in which they shared their sexual fantasies. Remember that I began the session with an exercise in which I insisted that you arouse your partner but never actually have sex. I also requested that your conversation about sexual fantasies not lead to actual sex. Refraining from sex helps rebalance the sexual power struggle. Now that you have control of your sex cycle and understand how to manipulate your lover so that he can complete it for you more fully, the time has come to have a satisfyingly good bonk!

If sex is still an issue in the relationship, a good session in bed will take more than jumping in between the sheets and letting nature take its course. You'll still need to stay in control if you are going to enjoy all of the delights that await you. Although you may feel horny from the exercises this week, you know that the wheels will quickly come off the wagon if he gets what he wants anytime he wants it! We know only too well that guys always seem to be ready for sex, while women have a more complex set of prerequisites that we need to get us emotionally and physically in the mood. His ability to switch on his love light at a drop of a hat can put a strain on your relationship. Everyday interactions, even innocent or genuinely tender gestures, may be a bit suspect because you might think that the reason he's being nice to you, giving you a playful squeeze or stroking your hair, is that he's after sex. You've been through the scenario all too often. He comes on to you, but you're not ready. So you either say no, and he gets hurt and reproachful, or you say yes, and *you* wind up feeling hurt and reproachful. It's a lose-lose situation.

Set a Day for Sex

I suggest that at this stage of retooling your relationship, you set aside one night a week for pure, no-holds-barred sex. It's only one night a week, but it's a very definite appointment that both you and he must honor. It is important that you do not have sex at any other time in the week. Having a specific time designated for sex takes the pressure off during the rest of the week. He knows he's going to get some, say, every Tuesday, so he can relax and stop working so hard by doing all of the wrong things to get you into bed. And you know you'll end up having sex that night, so you can set aside any suspicion that he is "on the make" when he gives you a cuddle. I've picked Tuesday, but it can be any day of the week. Make it definite, and stick to it.

Men often don't like the idea of a timetable, but you are in control now and have the power to drive the negotiation. Tell him that if he wants to be sure of getting sex, it will have to be on the day you prescribe. Of course, it is crucial that you fulfill your side of the bargain, no matter how you feel come Tuesday. The payoff is that you can rest assured that for the rest of the week there will be no sex, so you can go to bed, relaxed and comfortable, and read that magazine, knowing that nothing is going to happen. He will put up with the arrangement because he knows for sure that he will be getting sex on Tuesday.

Now that the sexual pressure is relieved, the much-needed affection that is so often lost when both of you are trying to deal with the problems in your sex life is able to reenter the relationship. Affection will flow back into your daily interactions quite naturally. You will find yourself able to caress him and accept his caresses without tensing up or hoping that these simple, friendly gestures won't have unintended consequences. Couples report that at this stage, a new energy is reintroduced and a heightened sense of closeness emerges.

EXERCISE

Make Love, Not Sex

The next and final exercise not only takes advantage of the gains you have made so far but also brings you full circle as you implement your control of your man to achieve greater sexual intimacy and satisfaction. It's really quite simple, and in a sense, you have already half completed the exercise, except that now I want you to do it again but this time without any physical constraints and you will finish the job! You might have already guessed that I'm going to ask you to revisit the first exercise you performed in this session, the one in which you freely touched your partner, exciting his senses. But this time I'd like you to combine this exercise with the act of making love.

Go back and re-create the activity you performed on your partner, whether it was a warm oil massage, bathing him in a scented bath, or tickling him with a feather. Tell him that you would like to be the Slave to his Master, and awaken his senses by touching him in new and exciting ways. This time, however, you can also switch roles. He can be your Slave, too. Let yourself go. Don't let him rush. You are in control and want each phase of your sex cycle to be fulfilled before you allow him to take it to the next phase.

With your aroused and heightened sense of awareness, gently and slowly move to his erogenous zones. Extend the sensate experience to these areas, as you move from the desire stage of your cycle to the arousal stage. When he reciprocates—and be sure to invite him to do so—bring the same attention and mindfulness to your own body that you did for his. He's simply doing what you taught him, so why not enjoy it?

In this delicious frame of body and mind, when you are ready, move to the plateau phase, linger there as long as you desire before climax, and finally enter the end phase, enjoying the new dimension of intimacy you have created.

Many of my female clients are so happy and excited by the results of their newly improved lovemaking that they say having great sex has repaired the relationship. If you are thinking along the same lines, I want to remind you that the good sex you are experiencing began while your clothes were still on. You can't have good sex without a good relationship. So take some of the credit, because you have single-handedly improved the communication between you and your lover that made possible the relationship's renewed sense of romance.

Greater Intimacy = Great Sex

I hope you listed a particularly generous indulgence as the eighth item on your reward list—something especially spicy and even a bit daring. Don't hesitate to give it to yourself. You earned it. It's your Romance badge.

Because you have improved the intimacy in other areas of your relationship, you are now able to dramatically heighten sexual intimacy and bring back the romance as well.

Jealousy: Avoid a Three-Way Collision

I am astonished every time a couple starts their first session by reassuring me that their problems lie outside the relationship and are not between the two of them. "Oh, no, Trina," they say, "the trouble with our relationship has nothing to do with us."

"It's not him," she confides. "It's his job. It's too demanding and high-pressured. It's pulling us apart."

"It's not her," he says, patting her hand, "it's her kid from her first marriage. The child is always crying and never leaves her alone."

They complain about clinging mothers-in-law, jealous ex-girlfriends, controlling brothers, or overly possessive friends. There may be friction with everyone and everything surrounding the relationship, yet the couple insists that everything between them is hunky-dory.

"No way, no how does the problem lie with either of us, Trina. We're just fine."

Yet it's clear to me from the outset that the couple is actually choosing to overlook the fact that they are willing accomplices to third parties who are hijacking their relationship and skewing the focus away from the real causes of contention.

Let's listen in to a typical first-time therapy conversation with a couple I'll call Taylor and Luis.

> Taylor: Luis comes home after a long day at work, I fix him something to eat, and he turns around and goes out to his mother's house, right away, before I've even had a chance to say hi. I've got nothing against Luis's mom. I love my mom, too, but why? I mean, why does she rely on her son night after night to fix her something to eat? I mean, she's a mom, she knows how to make a meal! He cooks for her more than he ever cooked for me. She says she has bad arthritis or migraine headaches or dizzy spells or whatever. But I've been around her enough to know she's putting it on a little too thick, if you know what I mean, to get her son to do things for her. Luis has a sister, so why doesn't his sister help out, that's what I'd like to know? And what's more—Luis and I don't agree on this, but I think his mom could do her own laundry if she wanted to, instead of relying on Luis to do it for her. And the shopping. And all of the little fix-ups around the house. Weekends? Don't even mention the weekends. I never see him. I might as well be single again.
>
> Luis: I know I've been spread too thin lately, going between my mom's house, the job, and being with Taylor. I know, and I've said so and apologized over and over again. But I've paid the bills on time, and we've gone out to the movies every Saturday night, and I fulfill my obligations as the man of the house in other ways, too. If that's not enough, I really don't know what more I can do. What more can I give? Unless she wants me to abandon my mother, and I know Taylor would never want that. I saw how my mom cared for my dad when he got sick, day after day, and how my mom cared for my sister and me. She did a good job, so I know it can be done.

You Can Be the Therapist

Because you've been carefully following these sessions, let's play a little game. I want you to assume the role of Luis and Taylor's therapist for a moment and look for clues about what's really going on. In other words, if you were the trained observer, what conclusions about Luis and Taylor's relationship could you deduce?

You might pick up on Taylor's complaint that Luis is never around, that he does things for his mom that he never does for Taylor. You might also hear a touch of reproach in her voice, almost as if she is accusing Luis of being duped, weak, and manipulated by his mother. In her remarks, I definitely hear that Taylor feels cheated, resentful that someone else is receiving all of Luis's attention and interest.

Listening to Luis, you might come to the conclusion that although he is a dutiful son, he is using the situation a bit aggressively, maybe even to get back at Taylor. It does seem that he could be letting his obligation to his mother become a way to avoid interacting with Taylor. It also sounds to me as if he feels put upon, a bit harassed and resentful of the demands Taylor makes on him. As we listen carefully to Luis, we also learn that when he was growing up, his mother spent a lot of time taking care of his chronically ill father. Luis acknowledges that his mother did a good job of splitting her time and attention between her husband and her children, but there is more than a possibility that Luis harbors a bit of resentment about the situation, as any child would who didn't have total and unconditional access to his or her mother's love.

As the weeks of therapy unfold, many of our initial observations are corroborated by additional comments the couple makes. Taylor's feelings of being deprived of Luis's affection rise to the surface. At one point, Taylor says, in a moment of anger, "If you think of yourself as such a good caregiver, why don't you start sending some of that caregiving my way! You're not a man, you're a mama's boy. If you were a man, you'd be spending more time at home giving me your love, instead of pampering that old woman."

Our hunch about Luis is also on target. Taylor's strident demands *are* driving him away. Here's what he says in reply to Taylor: "All I ever hear around the house is 'Luis, where are you going, why don't you stay home?' Or 'Luis, let's go out tonight, you never take me out,' when you know perfectly well that isn't true. God, sometimes you sound just like my sister. 'Do this for me. Do that for me.' Can't you understand that my mom is getting on in years? Can't you respect that this is my mother you are talking about? The woman who gave me life. You've just got to back off, bitch!"

You can imagine the fireworks that followed!

Taylor's story is that she was brought up by a single mom. Taylor's dad was an alcoholic and abandoned the family when Taylor was five. Her mom held down two jobs, leaving Taylor to raise herself when she wasn't being dropped off at the neighbor's. So when it came time for Taylor to construct her lens sentence, I could have almost written it for her. She wrote, "I am frightened of being abandoned and left behind, discarded and forgotten."

Taylor's lens sentence was activated each time Luis went off to care for his mother, because feelings arose that were reminiscent of those in her life when she struggled with the loneliness caused by her father's departure. When she constructed her artworks (session 2), she felt conflicted about where to put the button representing her mother; she told me that she longed to be close to her mother but knew in reality she wasn't. And when she added Luis and his family to her Present Patterns Artwork, Taylor placed an old, raggedy cloth button between her button and Luis's, to represent his intrusive mother.

When I helped her express her feelings using the XYZ communication exercise from session 5, what she said confirmed the hypothesis: "When you go off to care for your mother, I have this fear that you'll never come back. If you'd spent less time with your mother and more quality time with me, it would help me believe and trust that you will come back." What Taylor meant by "quality time," of course, was "intimate time." And as we know, intimacy is something that men often find very threatening.

Luis indicated in subsequent sessions that any hint of intimacy was closely associated with an earlier and very unhappy time in his life. As we know, Luis's mother spent a lot of time attending to his father's needs, time that Luis felt should have been spent on him or at least shared more fairly. The reference to his sister was a bit more hidden but turned out to be pivotal. Luis was the elder of the two children and had been made responsible for his sister's needs when their mother wasn't available. He cooked for her, washed her clothes, took her to school, and made sure she did her homework; in short, he played the role of the mother. Every demand that his sister made on Luis required him to take time away from activities with his friends or from attending to his own affairs. The kind of behavior that Taylor asked of him triggered feelings of being deprived of the pleasure-seeking activities he had missed when he was growing up. It also generated feelings of inadequacy stemming from his having the responsibility of raising his sister placed on his shoulders.

You might have already guessed that Luis's lens sentence was very similar to Taylor's: "I am fearful that I'll be left alone to fulfill the demands and needs other people put on me." Both Taylor and Luis are afraid of being abandoned, emotionally isolated, and deserted. In Taylor's case, she is looking to her partner to fill the role of rescuing her, by giving her the comfort she longs for and deserves.

For Luis, his dread of being abandoned is compounded by his fear of having emotional demands made on him. It is ironic, isn't it, that Luis finds himself reenacting his childhood scenario? Except that now he has cast himself in his mother's caregiving role, treating Taylor the same way his mother treated him, depriving her of love and affection the same way that it was withheld from him as a boy. This revelation became clear to him later on, when he talked through his genogram with me.

Read Luis's XYZ sentence and see whether you can sense the fear that arises when he confuses intimacy with the pain of having emotional demands made on him: "When you ask me to spend more time with you, it makes me feel all caged in and even panicked, so next time when you want me to hang with you, I would like you to wait for an opportunity for me to come to you."

This is not a very amicable solution from Taylor's perspective! All of the power to resolve her anxiety is squarely in Luis's control. What eventually happened was that Taylor performed the String Theory exercise and let Luis go to his mother's when he wanted, without Taylor pleading or complaining. By letting her string out, something quite miraculous happened. Not only did Luis get his XYZ sentence fulfilled, he began to pursue Taylor! He didn't feel hemmed in by her continual nagging for attention. He felt less and less threatened when he was around her, gaining the confidence that he wouldn't be responsible for her. She was controlling her string perfectly. He began to come out of his "cave" and feel more relaxed with her. He brought her small presents for no reason. He instituted "date night," in which every Tuesday they would plan on going out to dinner. Previously, Taylor was denied her emotional bucket for caregiving. All of the caregiving was done by Luis. Previously, Luis rebuffed Taylor's attempts at showing him affection. He misinterpreted them as emotional demands, requiring some form of reciprocity for him to show affection in return. As balance was restored in the relationship, her caregiving bucket began to fill, as he relinquished its sole control and accepted her caregiving activities without fear or panic.

Lo and behold! In a very short time, Luis was performing exactly as Taylor prescribed in her XYZ dialogue. Luis began to spend less time with his mother and more time with her.

The Other in Your Relationship

The "mother-in-law syndrome" that Taylor experienced with Luis is quite common. The third parties may be mothers-in-law, but they can also be friends and family. These intrusions don't even have to be people; they might be activities and other time commitments,

such as work, hobbies, or Internet games. A couple can use anyone
or anything to avoid the real issues plaguing their relationship. In
the case of Luis and Taylor, it wasn't really the mother-in-law who
was the issue; she was merely the means by which he could safely
communicate his dissatisfaction with the relationship.

Third parties are often considered by a member of the couple
to be intruders in the relationship. Yet the truth is, triangles occur
because the man and the woman find it difficult to confront the
crisis in their relationship and they discover the usefulness of bringing in a third party to dilute or lower the intensity of their struggle.
It is a strategy of diversion, a means by which couples sidestep their
problems, rather than face them head on.

It is not surprising that couples bring in third parties because the
prospect of dealing directly with their issues is terrifying. The only
two possible outcomes available to a couple encountering what they
believe to be an irresolvable problem is that they either settle it or
break up. So the guy and the girl unconsciously collude with each
other to bring a third party into the mix. The third party—whether
it is a person or an activity, such as work—helps lower the intensity
and enables the couple to argue about someone or something else
that doesn't directly threaten the relationship.

When a couple's struggle involves a third party, there are endless
ways to respond. The pressure to confront and settle the real cause of
friction is deferred. A third party creates a kind of distorted stability,
characterized by the couple's going around and around the problem
and getting nowhere, continually having the same skirmishes without resolution. It is much easier to argue with your husband about
his mother being so intrusive than to have it out with him for not
being strong enough or protective enough about your relationship
to keep his mother out of the picture.

Some triangles are only too obvious, as in the case of Taylor, Luis,
and Luis's mother. Taylor had no difficulty identifying the trouble-
some third party in that triangle. Remember Lisa from session 7?
It was easy for her to identify Tony's lover in his extramarital affair

as the third party in her triangle. Intrusions by third parties are often accompanied by feelings of jealousy. A nagging feeling that your man is spending too much time and attention on someone other than you is the telltale sign that a third-party triangle is having a destructive influence on the relationship. Is it his brother, who is over for dinner so often he's practically a roommate? Or his gang of friends with whom he went to school and hung out during the summers? Is it his ex—just a friend now but on the scene a little too often for comfort? If you feel jealous, it is often a reliable warning that you are in a triangle.

Triangles are relatively easy to spot when the role of the third party is played by a person. But as we have seen in previous sessions, some third parties are not people at all but instead activities that one person engages in so obsessively that it threatens the stability of a relationship. Does your boyfriend disappear every night to the basement to practice his guitar, instead of spending time with you? Does he spend weekends in the garage rebuilding the engine of that '67 Mustang he's been working on for more than a year? Does he play computer games into the early morning hours, instead of going to bed at the same time that you do?

Remember, anyone or anything can be part of your triangle when it is used by one or both of you to misdirect attention away from the obstacles that get in the way of the two of you achieving intimacy. Another way to think about it is that three of you are in the relationship: you, him, and it. As I have said, "it" can masquerade as a legitimate hobby or pursuit. Your partner may display a true passion for "it." He may be rehearsing forty hours a week in a band in the hope of getting a record deal. He may be writing after dinner every night, fueled by dreams of publishing his novel. He may be out early every Saturday morning riding twenty miles on his bike.

"It" can be an illness, an addiction, or a habit. "It" can come in many shapes and may be camouflaged and difficult to identify. Is your man always finding a new hobby—this week football, last week karate—all of which are expressions of his endless energy, or does he simply fill his calendar with sports and appointments so that he won't have to be with you? Ultimately, you are the judge, and if you are feeling cheated, regardless of the legitimacy of the object—whether a person or an activity—then how you feel is a valid complaint.

One of the most common ploys I encounter when helping couples is that one member uses his or her job as a smoke screen to hide behind, rather than confront the issues in the relationship. Remember Tanya and Peter from session 4? Tanya worked incessantly. It consumed her. She had her reasons: she had to work extra hard in a workplace filled with men; her boss was exceptionally difficult; it was a competitive position, and she wanted to be a vice president by the time she was thirty. It all makes sense and seems quite reasonable, except, as we know, she was simply dodging the issues that stemmed from her relationship. She also used the long hours with her team at work to avoid triggering her lens sentence, which was, "I am afraid to be on my own." Her job was her dodge, her feint, the third party in her relationship.

You Are Already Compromising Too Much

When your man seizes an "it" for his triangle and does so with enormous enthusiasm and zeal, then stepping between him and his passion can be extremely nerve-racking. How can you begrudge your partner his passion? It is awfully difficult for you to admit that he is cheating on you with an activity, a hobby, or a project, rather than with another woman. "But, Trina," you ask, "isn't sacrifice what lovers are supposed to do for each other? Shouldn't I put my own needs to one side to help make my man a success? Isn't being in a relationship all about compromise?"

I think you know me well enough by now to guess what my reaction is going to be: "Nonsense!" Compromise is not the answer, especially if you feel that you already have the short end of the stick and want more of his affection and attention. It really doesn't matter whether he is truly passionate about his "it" or he is merely using it to avoid the problems in his relationship. The answer, really, is immaterial. You know what you want, and, right now, you're not getting it from the relationship. Don't settle. You're his true love, his number one priority, and he's got to make room for you at the top spot. Stop making excuses for him. By playing into the triangle mentality, you are stopping yourself from getting what you want in a relationship. You want him, and if he can't manage it, then he can't have you.

Are You Triangulating the Kids?

There is another third party I haven't talked about yet, which can be one of the most volatile, ruinous, and tragic forces in a relationship, if not recognized and approached with care: children. Many times children become the third party in contentious relationships. Vulnerable and helpless, children are often used by a couple to deflect the pain of confronting issues about themselves or their relationship. Naturally, it's not something any couple wants to do intentionally, but it happens all too frequently and can have devastating consequences.

The child might be from a previous marriage or relationship of one member of the couple or from their marriage to each other. Yet because the couple is so embroiled in the dynamics of their relationship, they will clutch at anything or anyone to avoid the pain, humiliation, and guilt that they would experience if they confronted their core problems head on.

In my practice, I've encountered very extreme cases in which one or both members of a couple use a child to redirect attention away from the couple's conflict. I remember a case in which the mother used her seven-year-old as a physical barrier, encouraging the child's night terrors as an excuse to bring him into the marital bed so that she could avoid having sex with her partner.

As I said, this is an extreme example of how a parent can bring a child, with quite destructive consequences for the child, into a triangle. I've seen many more examples in which a couple's manipulation of their children is more subtle and therefore more difficult to identify. Children may be naive, but they have an uncanny ability to detect tension in a relationship, sensing when their parents are annoyed or emotionally hurt. Children are emotionally invested in having their parents happy and content. Not only do they abhor having someone they love in pain, but if the parents are secure, then the child also feels secure.

Think back to when you were a child and your parents argued. Wouldn't you have done anything to get them to stop and make up with each other? Do you remember how you felt when your father made your mother angry or sad, cry or yell? Or how it hurt you when your mother's constant nagging drove your father into his shell?

When parents begin to drift apart, their child, sensing an impending catastrophe, often displays behavior that, either for good or ill, is intended to bring them back together. One common set of behaviors displayed by older children is that they get into trouble with the law or get into drugs, in an unconscious hope that the energy used by the parents to attack each other will be redirected at them.

Let me give you another, more detailed example of how a child can play a pivotal role in a couple's triangle.

Miles is the three-year-old son of Susan and Jake. Susan and Jake had been married for about a year when they began to feel dull, bored, and frustrated because the excitement of their romantic honeymoon period had come to an end. That's when Miles came along. For a while, the relationship took on a fresh and exciting dimension with a series of elaborate family celebrations that lasted months. But during the last six months or so, the familiar dull and bored feeling once again settled in. It wasn't an overt feeling or something that either of them could quite articulate. Susan started by nagging Jake that he should share more of the child-rearing duties. Jake made a few badly timed comments about how Susan needed to lose more weight.

That's when Miles began to act up. He brazenly disobeyed his parents, refused to go to sleep, and threw violent tantrums, erupting in endless fits of kicking and screaming. Susan was at her wits' end. The child simply wore her down. At the end of an afternoon of sheer torture, all she could say was, "Just you wait until your father comes home. I will tell him how bad you've been!" When Jake came home and heard how awful Miles had been, he punished the child and sent him to bed without his bedtime story. At this point, both Susan and Jake were united, brought together in their anxiety and frustration over their disobedient son.

A little later in the evening, Susan snuck up to Miles's room and read him a bit from his favorite book because she knew he was still awake and wouldn't get to sleep without being read to. Now the triangle had shifted. It was Susan and Miles against Jake. Still being unable to sleep, however, Miles came downstairs after about an hour. Jake, feeling guilty for punishing his son, tried to make it up to the boy by playing together with his train set. Getting Miles worked up before bedtime was strictly against Susan's rules, so now the triangle had shifted again. It was Jake and Miles against Susan. The night came to an unhappy end when Susan discovered Jake and Miles playing video games, argued with Jake for keeping Miles up past his bedtime, and angrily sent Miles back to bed.

Recognizing Your Third Party

My guess is that by now, you've probably already begun to identify at least one triangle in your relationship. They are not hard to find, and almost every relationship has at least one. To see how your triangle fits into the larger picture of your relationship dynamics, I'd like you to do the following writing exercise.

• •

Open Your Notebook

In your notebook, list all of the possible third parties that come between you and your man. They could be people or activities you have already identified in previous sessions. Or maybe a new one comes to mind, now that you are more aware of the roles a third party can play in your relationship. Think back over the last few weeks, and identify the times that you felt a twinge of jealousy or were hurt when your partner excused himself to spend time with another person or activity instead of with you. Those moments, when your heart felt that little pinch, are a big sign that there is probably a triangle at play in your relationship. Here are some common distractions that you may recognize as candidates for your triangle:

- Excessive loyalty to family members
- Long and extensive periods of time spent working out
- Filling all free time with volunteer work in the community
- Compulsively playing games on the Internet
- Always fixing things around the house
- Overly occupying himself with a hobby or a sport
- Focusing exclusively on the children
- Allowing work to completely engulf his life
- Making every weekend night party time with his pals
- Having an affair

Now flip back through the pages of your notebook, and find your notes or photos of your artworks. You probably haven't looked at them in a long time, so spend some time reviewing all of the players and their relative positions on your life's stage. When you try to identify your triangles, they may not show up in your artworks as neat geometric shapes, so you'll have to broaden your conceptualization so that not all triangles have sides that are the same length. Remember Wayne and Sally from session 2? Sally put Wayne far away from herself and her children and put Wayne's sister-in-law between the two of them. In this case, Wayne represented one point on the triangle, Sally formed the second point, and Wayne's sister-in-law was the third point.

Reviewing your artworks is helpful in identifying not only third parties in your immediate love life but also in recognizing third-party patterns among your family members, both past and present. The "it" triangles in the artworks require a bit of detective work on your part. You can spot clues indicating some kind of disruptive force at work when people who should be in close proximity to one another are placed far apart. Gambling, alcoholism, womanizing, or simply an inability to settle into family life may be difficult "its" to spot, unless you have prior knowledge from your artworks or from your genogram or are able to dig around and ask a family member. Be prepared to put your detective hat back on and ask questions. Believe me, patterns will emerge from your artworks and genogram that will embolden you to seek out answers to what had been up to now unexplained or simply not talked about triangular interactions. Don't be surprised if you start to notice triangles popping up among the most unexpected family members and seeing how they relate to you and your relationships.

• •

Human beings are gluttons for punishment, especially self-punishment. We much prefer the very real anguish and torment that we create by avoiding our relationship troubles, rather than the imagined consequences of dealing with them head on. But now you have learned how to recognize and alter key emotional components in your relationship, and you have made enormous strides in learning to master the dynamics of your relationship. By working through the exercises thus far, you have acquired the tools and the experience you need to confront the gridlock in your relationship. Now it's time to take the next step by secretly controlling not only your guy but also the third party. To do this, you need to learn how to break the emotional and psychological bonds that hold your triangle together.

The Drama Triangle

As you now recognize, triangles are very tricky because they serve the purpose of stabilizing a relationship, although in a harmful and ultimately unsustainable way. That is why they are so hard to break. You've already taken the first step by recognizing when a third party is intruding in your relationship and blocking your path to intimacy. The next step is to "de-triangle" your relationship by understanding more deeply the forces at play in the triangle. Let me explain.

Each person in a triangle plays a certain role at any given time. That role is just like a part in a play, except that the play is your real-life drama. The importance of roles in a relationship should be familiar to you. In session 6, you saw how modifying your behavior by changing your role caused a transformation in your man's behavior toward you or, in short, changed his role. Observing and recognizing your behavior and then strategically altering it put you in control and changed the dynamics between you and your lover. Now I am proposing that you do something very similar, except that here you need to identify and understand the roles that are being played, not only by one person, but by two—the two other points of your relationship triangle.

Experts who study these interpersonal phenomena have found that there are three basic types of roles being played out at any given time between the three members of the "drama triangle."

Experts label these three sets of behaviors differently, but they all can essentially be characterized as the Persecutor, the Victim, and the Rescuer.

Persecutors are quick to blame others when things don't go according to plan. They are hypercritical and always see the negative. When things go wrong, they lose their temper. Persecutors are rigid and tend to see everything in black and white. They are authoritarian and like to set rules and limits unnecessarily.

Victims are quick to blame themselves when things don't go according to plan. They feel helpless and guilty, powerless and ashamed. When bad things happen, as they invariably do, they assume it is their fault. They constantly second-guess themselves; they feel badgered and put upon. The world and everyone in it is out to get them. In an argument, they see themselves as the injured parties and take a kind of pride in their suffering.

Rescuers have the belief that they can absorb blame and magically make situations all better for the Victim. Rescuers see themselves as champions, redeemers, and heroes, when, in fact, they avoid taking action. They keep Victims dependent and give them permission to fail.

Identify Who's Playing What Role

It would be a simple matter of identifying the Persecutor, the Victim, or the Rescuer if your life were a movie. In movies, people say and do things that make them easily recognizable. The Persecutor says, "You idiot, you're always getting it wrong!" The Victim quietly shoulders the abuse and mutters, "Yes, you're right, you're absolutely right." And the Rescuer swoops in and offers romance to provide the happy ending. But real life—your life—isn't like that. It's more subtle and restrained. Feelings of blame can be communicated by a crushing glance of reproof. A person's victim status is telegraphed by a dejected slouch of the shoulders. The promise of salvation comes in the form of a misinterpreted compliment by a new boss.

Identifying who's playing the role of Persecutor, Victim, or Rescuer in your drama triangle is made even more problematic because one person can play all three roles in a single occasion. Remember Susan, Jake, and their son, Miles? At one point in the evening, Susan was the Victim and her son played the Persecutor (yes, children are capable of making you feel blameworthy and helpless). The Victim role shifted when Jake came home and punished Miles, shifting the role of Rescuer to Susan, who snuck upstairs to read Miles a section of his favorite book. The roles of the triangle shifted again when Susan assumed the role of Persecutor (a bit harsh, but you get the point) when she had to mete out discipline on discovering her husband and son playing with the train set.

The roles in a drama triangle are seldom static; they shift and move. Adding to this already complex dynamic, each of these roles relies on the others to be effective. To fulfill the role of Persecutor, the Persecutor needs a Victim who will let himself or herself be persecuted. To play the part of a Victim, the Victim requires a Persecutor to act cruel to him or her. To be a Rescuer, the Rescuer needs a Victim to save. In other words, each role needs its negative complement in order to exist and for the triangle to achieve its special brand of corrosive stability.

Yet imagine what would happen if this interdependence could be interrupted. As a result, the drama triangle would be broken.

Detect the Roles You Play

The fact is, as you have followed the course laid out in this book, you probably have practiced and strengthened your ability to change your behavior and break free of roles you were playing with your lover. Remember in session 4 when you basically said, "'Night, babe, see you when I see you," as he left the house to go drinking with the boys? You were letting out your string, rewriting your role, shifting from Pursuer to Distancer. Now you need to assume that same mind-set and apply it to your drama triangle.

The key here, as it has been all along, is to use your ability to objectively observe what is really and truly going on and avoid getting suckered into acting on your lens sentence. Detaching yourself from the fray will prevent you from getting pulled into a vortex of emotionality. It worked with your code word back in session 5. It can work again here. Slow things down, dissect the dialogue, interrupt the flow. Sound familiar?

You have to disassociate yourself long enough to discern whether what is being said is making you feel helpless or hopeless, whether it's critical and abusive—in short, whether your partner is playing the Persecutor card. Remember, he can't persecute if you refuse to play the Victim.

Similarly, if you find yourself criticizing your man, feeling blind rage at his flagrant inability to respect a simple request like taking out the garbage or separating the recyclables, then pull back and check out what you are doing. Not only are you acting as the Persecutor, but you are also relating to him as if he's the Victim. Take control. Change your approach. Use your communication skills to defuse the situation, alter roles, and break your triangle. Here's an example of what I'm talking about.

Many women bond to their men out of a desire to rescue. Have you heard the saying "Men marry women hoping they won't change and women marry men hoping they will"? I've met many women who are practically obsessed with their role as Rescuer, risking their personal social networks and professional success to save their men from alcohol, drug abuse, or a downward spiraling career. They soon discover that although it is possible to play a part in supporting another person's rehabilitation, it's a lost cause to believe you can do it single-handedly.

If you suspect that you are playing the role of Rescuer, check it out by listening to what you say and how you say it. Are you making promises you can't keep and probably don't truly believe yourself? Are you complicitly making it possible for your man to perpetuate his destructive habits and ensure your role as Rescuer and his dependence on you? Phrases like, "No matter what you do, I'll always love you." Or, "Trust me, I can help you through this." Or, "Let my love help you get to where you want to go." These may be well intentioned on the part of the Rescuer, but they enable the Victim and are counterproductive.

• •

Open Your Notebook

Spend the next few days carefully listening to and closely watching your interactions with your guy; record in your notebook those moments when you feel yourself falling into the role of Persecutor, Victim, or Rescuer. Be sure to capture who played which role, what was said that caused you to act out the role, and what happened after you reacted. Following are examples from some couples I have worked with.

Sean has asked Lela whether she wanted to go out clubbing with friends on Saturday night, and Lela said she didn't want to. When asked why not, she replied rather tersely, "Just because. That's why."

Here's what followed:

Sean: You never want to go out anywhere and have fun. You are the reason I'm losing my friends. You can be such a bore. Name the last time we went out together and you actually enjoyed yourself.

Lela: You're much better with people than I am.

Sean: It's no big deal to be pleasant. You just don't try.

Lela: If it's so important to you, just go and have fun without me! If you want to get drunk and act stupid, it's fine with me.

Sean: Friends are what it's all about, Lela. They are important
   to me and should be important to you. Friends help you
   when you are down and make you feel good about yourself. Why don't you want to feel good about yourself?
Lela: Okay, okay, go! I want you to have fun. I'll figure out
   some way to fill the time, go to a movie or something.
Sean: (Sighing) No, it's okay. We'll stay at home. It's probably just as well.

In this case, Sean shifted from Persecutor to Victim, and
Lela, playing on Sean's guilt, shifted from Victim to Persecutor.
The third party, Sean's friends, were held up as Rescuers, giving
Sean a way to avoid having an intimate evening with Lela.

Here's how the conversation might have gone if Lela had been
prepared to depart from these roles and break the triangle.

Sean: You never want to go out anywhere and have fun.
   You are the reason I'm losing my friends. You can be
   such a bore. Name the last time we went out together
   and you actually enjoyed yourself.
Lela: You're much better with people than I am.

At this point, Lela hears that she is putting herself down,
playing the Victim, and chooses to take another approach. She
remembers her lens sentence and the XYZ exercise. Here is
how she might respond to control her man and the situation
to her satisfaction.

Lela: Look, I know it's important to you. But these large
   social situations make me feel, frankly, a bit awkward
   and on display.
Sean: You're no more on display than anyone else. And so
   what if you are? What's to prevent you from spending
   time and bonding with my friends?

Lela: Okay. When there is so much activity and noise, you often forget that I'm there. And it makes me feel uncomfortable when we are together on the dance floor that everyone is watching. So next time, I'd like it if you kept me close to you and that we only dance a couple of times.

• •

The Courage to Be Yourself

We have worked together throughout this book to give you control of your partner and your relationship so that you can achieve a higher degree of satisfaction and intimacy. The observation and conversational skills you have acquired can be used in any relationship with a third party. Naturally, it takes greater skill to operate in a situation that involves three forces instead of two, but the elements and the skill sets are the same.

You may have noticed that this session has been a bit different from the others leading up to it. It is as much about negotiating the challenges that are a constant in a relationship as it is about addressing issues that are currently disrupting your relationship. The potential for jealousy to threaten the balance is always lurking, as long as you are in the relationship. But now you know how to navigate a three-part relationship by solving problems, instead of creating drama and chaos; by facing painful situations honestly, rather than dodging, deflecting, or blaming others; and by having the courage to be more self-aware, instead of perpetuating your illusions. It's all part of having a grown-up, sustaining, and rewarding relationship with the person you love. The secret of controlling your man to achieve a more fulfilled, honest, and mature relationship is gaining control of yourself.

Congratulations! You've achieved tremendous progress in this session and deserve the gift that you've chosen for yourself as your ninth badge, the ninth reward on your list. It represents your Courage badge.

You are very near the end of this course of retooling therapy and have made enormous strides by following the prescriptions in this book. I am sure you are already enjoying greater intimacy with your partner, as well as a newfound feeling of freedom and independence. You now know how to recognize situations and behaviors that activate your lens sentence, and you've acquired the skills to master those behaviors and avoid those situations. Just as important, you know the secret of your man's lens sentence, which gives you the mechanism to control situations and behaviors to create greater intimacy.

By now, you probably have guessed the real secret behind my therapy. This book has been as much about you as about your lover—because the real key to retooling your relationship begins with retooling the attitudes and roles that you have acquired through the years.

• • • • • • • • • • • • • • PART THREE • • • • • • • • • • • • • •

Change to Retool Your Relationship

• •

Can You Commit?
Or Is He Just a Tool?

Many books about relationships begin with the topic of commitment. This one ends with it.

You may have wondered why I didn't begin our journey together by telling you where we were headed. Why not offer, at the outset of the expedition, a glimpse of the place where I hoped we end up?

But that would be a misleading way to begin the book, as it would be in therapy.

You began our work together eager for change, excited to start a rich and satisfying relationship. But what you didn't know then (and do now) was that without the necessary tools and practice in using them, you wouldn't be ready or able to accomplish the task. And how could you? You hadn't yet experienced and internalized the key concepts that were required to make a realistic assessment of where you truly wanted your relationship to go. There were still many illusions and self-delusions that needed to be debunked before you could envision the kind of relationship that you truthfully desired. As you worked your way through the concepts and the exercises in this book, you were preparing for an awareness that would pave the way for realistic and lasting change.

What kinds of change? Take, for example, the way you now communicate and enable your partner to communicate. Your newfound ability to recognize and break away from self-defeating patterns of behavior in your current relationship. The broader palette of emotions you are now free to express. The skill to observe and choose to act, instead of merely reacting on an impulse. These changes and the many others you have experienced throughout this book were necessary before any meaningful discussion of commitment could take place or even make sense.

The marvelous, magical value of any therapy is that very often you are unaware that it's at work, altering your perspective, shifting the way you feel about things, providing you with new behaviors and emotions to try on for size. The "work" of therapy continues around the clock, not only in the hour I spend with clients in my office. That's why the kind of therapy I give achieves results rather quickly and why the exercises in this book have an effect long after you stop reading. I often compare this phenomenon to what happens when you place a rock under the tire of a car stuck in the snow. The therapy provides the leverage that enables your relationship to gain traction and send the car moving under its own power down the road.

If you have taken to heart the ideas and the exercises presented in this book, you will have probably already noticed many changes in yourself, your partner, and your relationship. Some changes might be so obvious that you're pleasantly shocked when you become aware of them, for example, when your guy suddenly, totally out of the blue (or so it seems), grabs you and gives you a big, fat kiss before leaving for work! Or when you do something entirely out of character, such as simply refuse to do the dishes and just let them pile up for a few days. Other changes might be more subtle and understated.

For example, you might be getting ready for a dinner party and he suggests that you change your jeans into something a bit more upscale. Before mastering your skills of observation, you might have interpreted the comment as criticism of the way you looked. But now you understand that his comment might have come from a desire to protect you from feelings of embarrassment at being too dressed down for the occasion.

. . . .

Open Your Notebook

Recognizing how you and your relationship have altered as a result of the concepts and the activities contained in this book will provide an important frame for our conversation about commitment. Here's an exercise to help you evaluate how far you've come.

Let's retrace our steps together through the last nine sessions. Open your notebook and review each session, beginning with session 1. Write a sentence, a phrase, or just a word about any changes you have observed in yourself, your man, or the relationship. When you are finished with session 1, go on to session 2 and repeat the process, reading your notebook entries and then writing down any reflections or ideas that simply occur to you. In the sections that follow I've provided some questions and ideas that might help generate some thoughts and observations.

Connect with Your Tool. Can you recall a situation in which you and your partner have assumed the role of Pursuer and Distancer? Have you been able to step back from a conversation you are having with him and objectively listen to what is being said? Observing your conversations, have you been able to recognize situations where you've alternated between playing the Parent, the Child, and the Adult in the dialogue? Have you been able to control your shift from a Parent or a Child to an Adult role? How did your man respond? Have you asked questions to help clarify what he meant by a particular comment, without assuming that you knew and to show him that you were listening? Check in with your sex wheel that you created in session 1. Are things running more smoothly, or is it still a bumpy ride? What area of your wheel has improved?

Break Past Patterns, Solve Present Problems. Locate the patterns in your relationship that are similar to those of other members of your present or past family members. What character traits of the people in your life today are similar to those of past family members? Have the patterns you saw in your genogram helped you understand a problem in your relationship? What was the most significant revelation from session 2? If you had to do your Present Patterns artwork today, would you change the characteristics of the object you used to portray your man? Would you reposition your partner? As you review your Fantasy Future artwork, ask yourself whether any part of it has now moved from fantasy to reality? Would you change it in any way if you had to create a Fantasy Future artwork now? Which parts of your Fantasy Future artwork are achievable, and which ones aren't?

Why Are You with Him? Identify three things about your partner that once attracted you to him but now leave you cold. Are these the same ones that you itemized in your notebook when you first read session 3? List some of the feelings you now have when your lover starts to misbehave, and check them against the list you wrote down previously. How do they compare? Review your lens sentence. If you had the opportunity, would you revise or alter it in any way? What emotions are triggered when you review your lens sentence now?

Romance and Intimacy: The Perfect Balance.
Think back over the last few weeks and identify a situation in which you practiced the String Theory. Would you change your string's material today from the one you chose when you first read session 4? Do you notice yourself responding differently when he lets out his string to distance you? Has your guy shown any pursuing behavior toward you? Has he "gifted" you recently by performing a sensual treat or given you something he knows you would like, without asking anything in return?

Arguing Effectively with Your Tool. Recall an argument you've had with your partner recently. Based on what you learned in session 5, how did you use your XYZ sentences to express your lens sentence and control his behavior? How did he respond? Was he able to appreciate your concerns, and were you able to tell him how you wanted him to behave? How many times did you have to use your code word to regulate the temperature of the argument until it reached a point where you could discuss the matter in a calm fashion? How have you been able to use your understanding of your lens sentence to regulate your arguments?

Share Your Roles in the Relationship. Revisit your list of uncomfortable behaviors that are brought on by your lens sentence and that trigger self-criticism. Do you respond today the same way you did when you first read session 6? Review the four questions in the Your Invisible Deal exercise. Recall a situation from the last few weeks where you exhibited an emotion or a behavior that you removed from one of his "buckets." What about an emotion or a behavior that he exhibited that you now recognize as one from your "bucket"?

How to Deal with Your Tool's Cheating. Write down your definition of cheating. Has it changed at all during the course of reading this book? If so, write down in your notebook how it has changed. If your partner has cheated on you, has your understanding of his lens sentence helped you cope in any way with the experience? Has an understanding of your lens sentence helped you better manage the situation? If the roles were reversed and you were to have an affair, jot down what you imagine your reasons might be. Write about how these reasons relate to your lens sentence. Write down your definition of trust. Do you trust yourself? Revisit session 7's list of qualities that you think are essential in a trusting relationship.

Sex: The Ultimate Power Tool. Write down in your notebook any recent instances when you felt that you compromised to keep the relationship on a steady keel. Are these examples of new compromises or a continuation of past ones? Revisit your sex wheel. How has it changed? Which spokes have evened out to give you a smoother ride? Which ones still remain at different lengths, giving you a problem? Think back to the last time you made love. How has your sex cycle changed during the last few weeks, since you finished session 8? How did your guy respond when you clearly communicated with him what you enjoyed and needed to have more of to fulfill your cycle? Have you gained the level of intimacy you need? Has your relationship's emotional landscape changed during sex? Do you find yourself or your partner behaving differently in bed? What new behaviors has your guy expressed before, during, and after sex? What about you? What are you doing differently?

Jealousy: Avoid a Three-Way Collision. Revisit the triangles you identified in session 9 that intruded into your relationship. What third parties have fallen off the list? From this list of third parties, separate the "people" from the "its." Write down in your notebook a recent incident in which you used your XYZ sentence to change your guy's behavior toward a third-party activity. Can you identify a recent situation in which you played at least two of the three roles in the Persecutor-Victim-Rescuer drama triangle? Can you re-create snippets of the dialogue when you were able to pull back, observe, and redirect the role you played in the conversation?

• •

The Two Types of Commitment

How do you define "commitment"? When I ask women to use that word in a sentence, many refer to an obligation they've promised to perform. They describe activities that are a bit unpleasant to carry out at the time but that lead to a satisfying result. For example, you may hate dieting, but you definitely enjoy fitting into a size 10 dress. You might wince every time you take a chunk of your weekly paycheck and deposit it into your savings account, but you'll certainly enjoy that Caribbean vacation. And sitting through night and weekend classes is definitely a pain, but won't it feel great to finally get that college degree? Therapists label this "constraint commitment."

CONSTRAINT COMMITMENT

Constraint commitment feels like a contract with the outside world. Couples who stay together for the sake of the children or for religious reasons exhibit constraint commitment. When times are tough, constraint commitment keeps a couple together through the hard times. Even if the couple fights continuously with each other (the Cat and Dog couple type), constraint commitment often keeps them from calling it quits and dissolving the relationship.

DEVOTIONAL COMMITMENT

"Commitment" also has another meaning. The word describes the stance of a person who performs an activity that gives immediate pleasure or satisfaction. For example, an individual might be committed to singing in a band, learning to swim, or taking art classes. This is called devotional commitment, because you are dedicated to the activity and find it personally fulfilling.

Devotional commitment is vital because it produces the kind of positive emotional bonds that help keep a couple together. It creates feelings of togetherness, allowing the couple to take pleasure in each other's company. A relationship that consists predominantly of constraint commitment usually doesn't create feelings of enjoyment or delight in shared experiences and is devoid of vibrancy.

The point to remember is that in a resilient and enduring relationship, both of these commitment types coexist, but in order for two people to enjoy their lives together, a healthy amount of devotional commitment needs to be in play.

● ●

Open Your Notebook

Your relationship probably has both strands of commitment weaving through it, binding it together. This exercise is intended to help you identify which is the predominant commitment type in your relationship. After reading the following lists, write down in your notebook five constraint commitments that you think are holding you in the relationship, the commitments you keep because they're your duty. In the second column, make a list of five devotional commitments, those activities you take pleasure in, look forward to, or are passionate about while you are doing them. Some activities may be in both lists. Here are some ideas to get you started.

Constraint Commitments

You are committed to staying with him because of religious beliefs.

You are committed to making the relationship work for the sake of the children.

You are committed to your guy because your family expects you to be.

You are committed to working long hours to pay the bills because he has lost his job.

You are committed to losing weight because you know he likes you better when you are thinner.

Devotional Commitments

You are committed to caring for your partner when he is sick.

You are committed to making a happy home.

You are committed to the promise you have made yourself to work out in the gym more often.

You are committed to walking your dog together with your partner.

You are committed to learning to salsa with your partner.

• •

Are You Ready to Commit?

Sometimes there is more involved in being ready to commit to a relationship than finding the right person to commit to. Sounds strange, I know, but I've had young married women sit across from me in therapy, desperate and despondent, because they had not been prepared to make the commitment when they did. A few months earlier, these young girls were blissfully happy because they each had found a perfectly compatible partner and then quickly, even blindly, got married. Now in therapy, they tell me they still love their men but regret the decision to marry.

A look at their lens sentence might have helped give them a clearer understanding of what was driving them to make this important decision. Many women feel that a committed relationship will cure their insecurity and fears of instability. One typical example from my practice was when a young woman, Melissa, gradually realized that she wanted some time for herself, time she needed to be young, carefree, and single. It took a great deal of courage to try to break away from her relationship because she was confronting her lens sentence head on. Yet each time she tried to call it quits with her boyfriend, he came back pleading, saying that he would die—yes, die—without her. And each time, she caved, because she was the one who secretly feared that she would die if she wasn't in a relationship. He was very good at activating her lens sentence to get what he wanted. She was able to leave him eventually, because she recognized that her lens sentence ("I am afraid of being left alone and excluded") was now in conflict with her true desires.

No one will give you permission to leave a relationship that isn't working or that you feel you're not ready for. The strength and resolve to change comes from within you, but now you have the tools to see more clearly the motivation that is driving your decision. It is my hope that you will use your lens sentence to understand the deep reasons you feel ready to commit. The tools that are now in your possession will give you the ability to discern between needing to be in a relationship and wanting to be in one, and the confidence to choose what's right for you.

Close Your Exits

My clients are always surprised by their first session with me because it's nothing like what they expect. They think that I'm going to make demands on them right away, shackle them to a prescribed list of do's and don'ts, and insist they follow a therapeutic plan. Nothing could be further from the truth. I always start therapy with the exit doors wide open, so that no one feels trapped or constrained.

When clients know that the exits are open, they enter into the therapy with a spirit of exploration and curiosity. It's a great way to start. Yet there comes a time in therapy—as in life—that the benefits of a relationship cannot be fully realized unless the exit doors are closed and the individual makes a commitment to the work and the benefits that lie ahead.

The time has come for you to shut the exit doors.

Commitment isn't a matter of degrees. It's an all-or-nothing proposition. There is no such thing as "total commitment" because commitment *is* total, absolute, unqualified. If you are really serious about retooling your relationship, you can't do it from the sidelines. Committing to a relationship is a bit like trust. You just do it.

Many of my clients insist on keeping their options open, making sure that an escape route is ready in case the retooling feels too risky, hopeless, or dangerous. But escape routes are the opposite of what commitment is all about. You can't honestly commit if you are always looking over your shoulder to see whether the back door is open. You've got to shut that door if you are going to fix your man. You can't keep planning your retreat from the work to which you've committed yourself. The only way for the "work" laid out in this book to work is for you to be sure that you have not left yourself avenues of avoidance. And remember: all relationships are work.

We live in such a disposable world. If we don't like something, we simply toss it and get another. Everything is so easily replaceable. There's a hole in your sweater? Buy a new one. Don't like the food you ordered? Send it back. Dissatisfied with the car you just bought? Trade it in. Tired of your job? Get another.

When a woman hits a tough patch in her relationship, it's tempting for her to feel as if there is always another gorgeous guy just around the corner. So she says to herself, "There are so many available, attractive, and terrific guys out there, why work so hard trying to fix this hopeless Tool who's trashing me all the time? Such a lying bastard. What a lazy cheat. Why break into a sweat and try to fix him, when I can just play the field for a while and pick up another, better guy who'll treat me right?" How many times have you said and done that, only to find yourself in the same position you are in now?

The fact is, if you chuck it all in and start over with another guy, you'll simply find yourself repeating the same scenarios, reliving the same dilemmas, and reenacting the same mistakes that you did with the previous guy and the guy before that and the guy before that. And if you get around to dumping this new guy you're so keen about, I guarantee that unless you retool yourself, you'll repeat the same drama with the next guy and with similar poor results. So, you see, it really doesn't matter who you are with. The lesson you'll eventually learn is that you need to *commit* to fixing yourself, your man, and your relationship, because that's the only way you'll ever be able to break free of the self-defeating patterns you've been trapped in. And the only way to really commit is to remove all of the exits.

• •

Open Your Notebook

For many couples, marriage is a logical extension of a committed relationship. I have discussed one way that the lens sentence can play a role in why a person might want to reconsider getting married. Yet the lens sentence can also help you crystallize other perceptions about marriage that might be helpful to you. If you are on your way toward fixing your man and you find yourself in a stable and committed relationship, try this exercise. The following list gives some of the reasons many people marry. Take out your lens sentence and place it next to each statement, in succession. In your notebook, write down any reactions or feelings that the juxtaposition of the two have triggered. For example, if your lens sentence is "I am afraid of being abandoned," what emotions surface when you read the statement "We want a place of our own"? Do you feel that leaving your current home and setting up house with your boyfriend will make it more difficult for him to leave you? Do you feel that having him in the same house and sharing a space with him will contribute to your sense of stability and security? Write these thoughts in your notebook.

Reasons Women Give for Marrying	*Thoughts That May Be Triggered*
"We want a place of our own."	• Moving in with him will make it harder for him to leave. • Living with him will encourage him to include me more fully in his life. • When we move in together, I'll be totally exposed. • I fear he'll discover and dislike the "real" me.
"Our financial situation will improve."	• By marrying him, I'll have more financial security and therefore less stress and worries. • If I lose financial independence, I'll also lose my identity.
"He proposed."	• I feel swept away by the excitement of being asked. • I fear disappointing him by giving any answer other than yes.
"I want to have children."	• Having a child together will bring him closer to me. • Having a child will somehow complete me and make me more of a woman.

Reasons Women Give for Marrying	*Thoughts That May Be Triggered*
"Getting married will improve the relationship."	• Getting married will provide the stability I need to get on with my life. • Getting married will enable me to do more of the things for him that I enjoy. • Getting married will show the world what a wonderful couple we are.
"It's about time."	• My parents were married and had me by the time they were my age. • Most of my friends are married, and it will be nice to be included among them.

• •

The Four Relationship Busters

You know firsthand how difficult and painful it is to change yourself, and now you also know that transforming yourself is the only way you can bring about the change you want in your man. The dynamics of interpersonal relationships are a miraculous process. They ensure that the change you create in yourself will automatically transform your partner as well. You saw the process in action in certain exercises, such as when you let out your string to distance him, only to have him rewind it and start to pursue you. Your understanding of how and why you act modifies the nature of your interactions with your partner. Any change within the relationship's interactions catalyzes a change in him. Nothing as foundational as altering the dynamics within a relationship happens quickly or painlessly, but I've seen it work on hundreds of couples. With patience and persistence, the process works.

Yet there are instances when women find that their relationships have deteriorated to such an extent that any attempt to revive them is futile. When this happens, no matter how hard the woman tries to communicate with her guy, she meets implacable resistance and a dead end. No matter how far she lets out her string, how many times she invokes her code word during an argument, or how clever she is in trying to take back emotions she has put in his bucket, the man is totally unresponsive, unyielding, and unfeeling. There are situations when change in the relationship is simply not possible.

There are four behaviors that spell danger for a relationship.

1. **Criticism:** Steady and relentless expressions of disapproval and censure. I have worked with couples where the men consistently viewed their partners as being hopelessly inadequate and always falling short of expectations. The man lords it over his woman in the role of the scolding parent. His verbal punches are aimed where he knows they will do the most harm. He is the Persecutor in the relationship, and his partner is cast as the perpetual Victim, unable to do right or achieve any level of success.

2. **Contempt:** Conveying disdain and disapproval of a partner, even a hatred. Here, the partner is openly scorned. Every attempt at giving pleasure or satisfaction is met with derision. The Victim is persecuted with enthusiastic fervor. The Persecutor tears away at the Victim's self-confidence with disdainful quips and remarks. An atmosphere of extreme disapproval of the partner is almost palpable.

3. **Defensiveness:** Unwilling and unable to tolerate any complaint or grievance. A man on the defensive is always

quick to imagine that he is being disrespected or offended. His armor is always up. He unfailingly puts the blame on someone other than himself—usually on his partner. He denies responsibility for any deficiencies in the relationship or any dissatisfaction his woman might feel.

4. **Stonewalling:** Deliberate and obstinate refusal to cooperate in any discussion. There are elements of criticism, contempt, and defensiveness in stonewalling behavior, but it is chiefly recognizable because of its extreme and excessive nature. Access to any but negative emotions is completely blocked off. Women with stonewalling partners often describe their men as conveying the attitude of "Talk to the hand, 'cause the heart ain't listening." It feels as if he has checked out of the relationship a long time ago. Women soon stop attempting to communicate with stonewalling men because trying to talk to them brings on feelings of self-deprecation. It's like talking to a wall.

If your guy is still displaying these behaviors, you may have unfortunately reached an impasse. After all of your attempts at communication, if he still refuses to show any signs of change, then it may not make sense to consider committing to the relationship.

The Choice Is Yours

As we look back over the last few weeks, the changes that you and your man have gone through are quite remarkable. Chances are, you are fighting less, and when you do, the arguments resolve in a rational and considerate way. You are experiencing parts of yourself that you had thought you lost forever. There is a new maturity to your relationship. You find that you don't need to nag him as often. When he acts threatening, unpleasant, or hurtful, you feel that you can get yourself heard. You feel more appreciated and have regained some trust. He understands your sexual needs, and your sex life is now back on track. Incredibly, he is now showing the very early but unmistakable signs of a renewed warmth and intimacy.

The relationship has improved. Life is better—and not only for you. The environment you have created provides him with the opportunity to safely express the pent-up emotions and needs he has tamped down for a very long time. His sex life is better. He is receiving the support and encouragement he naturally desires. He is able to be more intimate without fear of losing his masculinity. He is thriving.

Or at least, he should be.

If he hasn't responded positively, then you might have to face a few difficult facts. If his stonewalling behavior has continued, and he has not curtailed his criticism, contempt, or defensiveness, then I'm afraid real trouble lies ahead as you decide whether you want to stay in such an abusive relationship. That's because you have brought the relationship to a point where you can't be the only one doing all of the work. I see clients whose relationships are so damaged that it is hard for me to hold out any hope for them. Sometimes a guy is just a Tool. The choice, ultimately, is theirs. If they want to stay together and work on being together, the only precondition, I believe, is that they both commit.

Your relationship now is on a new plane, and you put it there. There are many wonderful new experiences in store for you and your guy. But remember in session 5 when I said that if you are in a relationship, you are in a struggle? There will be episodes of frustration and resentment, periods of pain and bitterness. Yet now you have the tools to navigate your way safely through these obstacles to a much calmer and sunnier place. The big difference going forward in your relationship is that he is now by your side.

If you have decided that your Tool is worth the work and the relationship has a future, if the progress you've made up to this point gives you reason to believe that your man can be reconditioned to give you what you desire and deserve, go ahead and award yourself the final gift on the list you made at the beginning of this book. You have earned your Commitment badge.

If you make an honest assessment of your man's ability to be changed and consider how much you've been through already, and then you decide that the time has come to part ways—congratulate yourself as well. You have earned a Commitment badge for yourself and your future. Enjoy your last and hopefully most enjoyable gift. By responsibly and thoughtfully deciding to break off the relationship, you have made as courageous a step forward in fulfilling your potential for happiness as if you had gone through the process and decided to stay with your boyfriend.

Up until now, you had to resort to subterfuge and secrecy to get your guy to change his behavior. Now, you don't have to do all of the work. You've brought him to the point where he'll begin to help you, because he is also the beneficiary of the relationship's renewed vigor and vibrancy. The relationship has shifted from combat to collaboration. You have surreptitiously taught him that a relationship is in constant flux and requires continuous adjustments. A new intimacy has arisen, because you have helped him be more expressive of his needs and desires. Your bonds are strengthened because of the emotions you now share.

You can never truly lose what you now know about yourself. Your lens sentence is a remarkable tool and is yours forever, to use as your compass as you navigate the daily challenges of love and life.

How you use it to fix your man, retool your relationship, and create a future of your design is now entirely up to you.

Further Reading and Web Sites

Further Reading

Hendrix, H. *Getting the Love You Want: A Guide for Couples*. New York: HarperPerennial, 1988.

Love, P., and S. Stosny. *How to Improve Your Marriage without Talking about It*. New York: Broadway Books, 2007.

Skynner, R., and J. Cleese. *Families and How to Survive Them*. London: Vermillion, 1997.

Web Sites

www.vh1.com/shows/tool_academy/season_3/series.jhtml

The official Web site of *Tool Academy*. Offers insider information and sneak peeks from the latest season and new recruits as well as an archive of past episodes. You can see the therapy techniques from this book in action.

www.trinadolenz.com

My official Web site. Find out more about my background and training, see photos and highlights from *Tool Academy*, and get the latest updates on my public lectures and appearances.

www.relate.org.uk

Relate is a center for excellence in relationship studies in the United Kingdom and is the institution where I received my professional training in couples therapy. Relate has a network of seventy-seven centers in more than six hundred locations throughout the United Kingdom.

www.bbc.co.uk/relationships/couples

A comprehensive site that gives advice on all aspects of relationships. Contains exercises and articles on many of the topics covered in this book.

www.smartmarriages.com/index.html

Official Web site of the Coalition for Marriage, Family and Couples Education. Many of the articles and services listed here pertain to marriage and relationship education, as well as coalition-supported training programs for relationship counselor professionals.

www.family-marriage-counseling.com

The U.S.-based Family & Marriage Counseling Directory provides a nationwide clearinghouse for counselors and therapists throughout the country. It also provides links to helpful articles and listings of public forums for advice and support, therapists who provide telephone and online counseling, and self-help programs for troubled marriages.

www.gettingtheloveyouwant.com

The official Web site for Imago Relationships International, cofounded by Harville Hendrix, Ph.D., and Helen LaKelly Hunt, Ph.D. The Imago Relationship approach has similarities to Relate's work in the United Kingdom and leverages many of the same key theories that I do in this book. Among the site's many features is a directory of Imago therapists, workshops, and products.

www.aamft.org

The official Web site for the American Association for Marriage and Family Therapy, the governing body for marriage and family therapy in the United States. The site contains links to books, training, and therapists.

References

Bowlby, J. *A Secure Base: Parent-Child Attachment and Healthy Human Development.* London: Routledge, 1988.

_____. *The Making and Breaking of Affectional Bonds.* London: Tavistock Publications, 1997.

Byng-Hall, J. "Scripts and Legends in Families and Family Therapy." *Family Process* 27: 1–8, 1988.

Catherall, D. R. "Working with Projective Identification in Couples." *Family Process* 31: 355–367, 1992.

Dicks, H. "Object Relations Theory and Marital Studies." *British Journal of Medical Psychology* 36: 125–129, 1963.

Greenberg, L. S., and S. M. Johnson. "Emotionally Focused Couples Therapy." (pp. 253–278). In Jacobson, N. S., and A. S. Gurman, eds., *Clinical Handbook of Marital Therapy.* New York: Guilford Press, 1986.

Jacobs, M. *The Presenting Past: The Core of Psychodynamic Counselling and Therapy*, 2nd ed. Milton Keynes, Berkshire, UK: Open University Press, 1985.

Laverack, J., and S. Laverack. *Perceptions: Working with Couples: Active Techniques.* Self-Published: Wales, UK, 1996.

Mason, B. "Towards Positions of Safe Uncertainty: Human Systems." *Journal of Systemic Consultation and Management* 4: 189–200, 1993.

Middleberg, C. V. "Projective Identification in Common Couple Dances." *Journal of Family Therapy* 27(3): 341–353, July 2001.

Ruszczynski, S. *Psychotherapy with Couples: Theory and Practice at the Tavistock Institute of Marital Studies.* London: Karnac Books, 1993.

Scarf, M. *Intimate Partners, Patterns in Love and Marriage.* Toronto: Ballantine Books, 1988.

Scheinkman, M., and M. D. Fishbane. "The Vulnerability Cycle: Working with Impasses in Couple Therapy." *Family Process* 43(3): 279–299, 2004.

Skynner, R., and J. Cleese. *Families and How to Survive Them*. London: Vermillion, 1997.

Stewart, I. *Transactional Analysis: Counselling in Action*. London: Sage, 1989.

Wile, D. B. *Couples Therapy: A Nontraditional Approach*. New York: John Wiley & Sons, 1981.

Willi, J. *Couples in Collusion*. New York: Jason Aronson, 1982.

————. *Dynamics of Couple Therapy: Understanding the Potential of the Couple-Therapist Triangle*. Washington, DC: Jason Aronson, 1984.

Index

abstinence, 191
affairs. See cheating (session 7)
anger, 106, 109–13
Are You Really Listening
    exercise, 25
arguments (session 5), 105–23
  assessment of change made, 229
  award for completing session, 122
  control in, 108–9, 114–18
  deeper meaning behind, 118–21
  introduction, 105–8
  practice exercises, 113–19
  tips for, 120–21
  XYZ sentences, 109–13, 115
arousal, sexual, 34–35, 184–85
artwork family relationship
    exercise, 44–54
  examples of, 48–49, 50, 52–53
  fantasy future, 60–62
  introduction, 44–45
  observations and reflections,
    50–54
  Past Patterns artwork, 45–47
  Present Patterns artwork, 49–50

third-party identification, 213
attachment, string theory of, 90–98
attraction, 64–65. See also reasons
    for being with him (session 3)

"Babes in the Woods"
    relationships, 12–13
Bad Feelings list, 72–73
badges
  Commitment, 242
  Communication, 37, 122
  Courage, 220
  Insight, 79
  Intimacy, 104
  Maturity, 147
  Romance, 199
  Trust, 173
betrayal, feeling of, 12, 157
button family relationship
    exercise. See artwork family
    relationship exercise

"Cat and Dog" relationships, 14
cheating (session 7), 148–74

cheating (session 7) (*continued*)
  assessment of change in
    handling, 230
  award for completing session,
    173
  definition of, 153–56
  in denial about, 157–58
  emotional toll of, 150–51, 162,
    169–70
  exercises, 162–64, 166–70
  finding out truth about,
    158–61, 163–64, 166–69
  forbidden fruit fantasy, 148–49
  prevalence of, 150
  rebuilding trust after, 170–74
  staying in or leaving relationship
    after, 164–65
  types of, 151–53
children
  conflicts over having, 41–42
  as third party in relationships,
    209–11
Child role, 27–30
code words, 116–18
commitment (session 10), 225–42
  award for completing session,
    242
  choosing, 240–41
  closing "exit doors" for, 234–36
  definition of, 231–32
  four relationship dangers,
    238–40
  readiness for, 233–34
  review of sessions, 227–31
  tools necessary for, 225–27
  types of, 231–32
Commitment badge, 242
communication
  as adult instead of parent or
    child, 28–31
  control over, 108–9

gender differences, 16–17
  importance of, 3–4, 36–37
  about intimacy needs, 94–95
  about sex, 186, 193–94
  stonewalling behavior, 240
  See also arguments (session 5)
"communication affairs," 152–53
Communication badge, 37, 122
compromise, 180, 208–9
connecting with tool (session 1),
    11–37
  assessment of change made,
    227–28
  conclusion and award for
    completing session, 37
  introduction, 11–12
  through listening, 21–27
  through observation, 17–19
  and past experiences, 20–21
  relationship types, 12–16
  roles in relationship, 27–30
  sex check-up, 31–36
  speaking different language
    problem, 16–17
constraint commitment, 231
Container exercise, 141–46
contempt, 239
Control Your Dance Exercise,
    96–97
Couple Fit exercise, 68–79
  connections and similarities
    between lists, 70–73
  emotions underlying, 75–77
  lens sentences, 77–79
  lists, 69–74
  overview, 68
Courage badge, 220
criticism, 239

defense mechanisms, 41
defensiveness, 239–40

desire, 183–84
devotional commitment, 232
domestic violence, 115–16

emotions
    Couple Fit exercise, 75–77
    defense mechanisms, 41
    and infidelity, 150–51, 162,
        169–70
    past experiences impact, 20–21
    and role-playing, 130–31, 133,
        140
    See also feelings
estrogen, 182
exercises
    arguments, 113–19
    cheating, 162–64, 166–70
    Couple Fit, 68–79
    fantasy future, 60–61
    genograms, 54–60
    intimacy, 92–93, 96–103
    listening, 22–25
    overview, 5–6
    roles in relationship, 29–30,
        133–40, 141–46
    sex, 191–94, 198–99
    See also artwork family
        relationship exercise;
        notebooks and notebook
        exercises
"exit affairs," 151–52
extroverts, 127–30, 133

family relationships
    artwork exercise, 44–54, 60–62
    genogram exercise, 44–45,
        54–60
Fantasy Future exercise, 60–62
feelings
    Bad Feelings list, 72–73
    of betrayal, 12, 157

inability to express, 140
    neutral expressions of, 109–13
    See also emotions
finances, control over, 176–78
forbidden fruit fantasy, 148–49
foreplay, 184–85

gender differences
    communication, 16–17
    intimacy, 84–87
    sex, 34–35, 180–87
genograms, 54–60
    connections, 58–60
    defined, 54
    drawing exercise, 56–57
    introduction, 44–45, 54–55
gift-giving exercise, 98–103
goal setting, 61–62

hobbies and leisure activities, 95,
    207

"Idol and Fan" relationships,
    13–14
infidelity. See cheating (session 7)
Insight badge, 79
Internet-based affairs, 154
intimacy (session 4), 83–104
    assessment of change made, 229
    award for completing session,
        104
    checkup, 103–4
    Control Your Dance Exercise,
        96–97
    examples of, 87–92
    introduction, 83
    vs. romance, 84–87
    string theory, 90–98
    Three Gifts exercise, 98–103
Intimacy badge, 104
introverts, 127–30, 133

Invisible Deal exercise, 137–40
Is He Cheating? exercise, 162–64
It's Your Turn to Rant exercise,
    169–70

jealousy (session 9), 200–221
    assessment of change in
        handling, 230–231
    and compromise, 208–9
    conclusion and award for
        completing session, 220–21
    denial of, 200–201
    example of, 201–5
    roles in drama triangle, 214–20
    third parties in relationships,
        205–14
jobs, 208

language, gender differences in,
    16–17. *See also*
    communication
leisure activities and hobbies,
    95, 207
lens sentences, 77–79
    and arguments, 119–21
    and commitment readiness,
        233–34
    and marriage reasons, 236–37
    and role-playing, 131–32
    and sex cycle, 188–91
    writing, 77–79
Let's Talk about Sex exercise,
    193–94
listening, 21–27
Listen to the Truth exercise,
    166–69
love/hate enigma, 70–71

Make Love, Not Sex exercise,
    198–99
marriage, reasons for, 236–38

"Master and Slave" relationships,
    14–15
Maturity badge, 147
memories, 20–21
money, control over, 176–78

notebooks and notebook exercises
    arguments, 118–19
    cheating, 155–56, 165, 172–73
    commitment, 227–31, 232–33
    Couple Fit, 68–70
    family relationship artwork
        exercise, 47
    listening, 21–22
    marriage reasons, 236–38
    money, 176–78
    observing relationships, 17–18
    relationship triangle roles,
        218–20
    rewards, 7–8
    roles in relationship, 30–31
    setting up, 6
    sex cycle, 33–34, 187, 188
    sex wheel, 33, 187
    third parties in relationships,
        212–13
    trust after cheating, 170–71
    XYZ sentences, 110–13

observation, 17–19
"opposites attract" myth, 41–42
orgasm, 35, 185–86

Parent role, 27–30
past patterns, breaking to solve
        present problems (session 2),
        38–63
    assessment of change made, 228
    changing, 40–41
    conclusion and award for
        completing session, 61–63

Couple Fit exercise, 74–77
family relationship artwork
    exercise, 44–54
family relationship genogram
    exercise, 44–45, 54–60
Fantasy Future exercise, 60–61
identifying, 39–40
impact on present relationships,
    20–21
introduction, 38–39
"opposites attract" myth, 41–42
repeating nature of past
    problems, 43–44
Past Patterns artwork, 45–47
Persecutor role, 215–16
physical attraction, 64–65. See also
    reasons for being with him
    (session 3)
Pipe Down and Listen exercise,
    22–25
plateau phase, of sex cycle, 185
porn, 154
power, in relationships, 175–80
Present Patterns artwork, 49–50
"Pursuer and Distancer"
    relationships, 15, 87–89, 90,
    94–95, 97

reasons for being with him (session
    3), 64–79
    assessment of change in
        thinking, 228
    award for completing session, 79
    examples, 66–68
    introduction, 64–66
    love/hate enigma, 70–71
    See also Couple Fit exercise
Recognize the Roles You Both Play
    exercise, 29–30
relationship blueprint, 77–79
relationship types, 12–16

reporting back, 26–27
Rescuer role, 215–16, 217
resolution phase, of sex cycle,
    186–87
rewards, for completing sessions,
    7–8
role reversals, 15
roles, breaking free of (session 6),
    124–47
    assessment of change made, 229
    award for completing session,
        147
    constraint of emotion/behavior
        buckets, 130–31, 133, 140
    exercises, 29–30, 133–40,
        141–46
    introduction, 124–26
    and lens sentences, 131–32
    parent/adult/child, 27–30
    relationship triangles, 214–20
    role-sharing goal, 126–28
    unexpected outcomes of,
        146–47
romance, vs. intimacy, 84–87
Romance badge, 199
rules of the game, 4–5

Sensual Touch exercise, 191–93
sessions, overview of, 5–6. See also
    specific sessions
sex (session 8), 175–99
    abstinence, 191
    arousal, 34–35
    assessment of change made, 230
    award for completing session,
        199
    communication about, 186,
        193–94
    exercises, 191–94, 198–99
    gender differences, 34–35,
        180–82

sex (session 8) (*continued*)
    Internet porn, 154
    mixed messages, 35–36
    as power tool for women,
       175–76, 178–80
    scheduling, 197–98
    sex cycle, 33–34, 182–91
    sex wheel, 32, 187
    and string theory, 104
sex cycle
    description of, 182–87
    and lens sentence, 188–91
    questionnaire, 33–34
sex drive, 181–85
sex hormones, 181–82
sexual fantasies, 193–97
sex wheel, 32, 187
SMART test for gift giving,
    101–2
stonewalling, 240
string theory, 90–98, 104
success, determinants of, 8

Ten Things I Hate about Myself
    exercise, 133–37
testosterone, 181–82
therapists, acting like when
    listening, 22–25

therapy
    Trina's style, 5
    value of, 226
third parties, in relationships
    children as, 209–11
    identification of, 205–8,
       211–14
    roles of, 214–20
    See also jealousy (session 9)
Three Gifts exercise, 98–103
"three-legged stool" infidelity, 151
time-outs, in arguments, 114–18
Tool Academy, 3–5, 35
tool kit, 6–8, 126
Tools, definition of, 2
trust
    importance of, 161
    rebuilding of, 164, 170–74
Trust badge, 173

Victim role, 215–16

XYZ sentences, 109–13, 115

Your Fantasy Future exercise,
    60–62
Your Invisible Deal exercise,
    137–40